CUTAWAY AIRCRAFT OF WORLD WAR TWO

ARGUS BOOKS

Argus Books
Argus House
Boundary Way
Hemel Hempstead
Hertfordshire HP2 7ST
England

First published by Argus Books 1989

ISBN 0 85242 993 2

Typeset by Gilbert Composing Services

Printed and bound in Great Britain by William Clowes Ltd. Beccles

INDEX

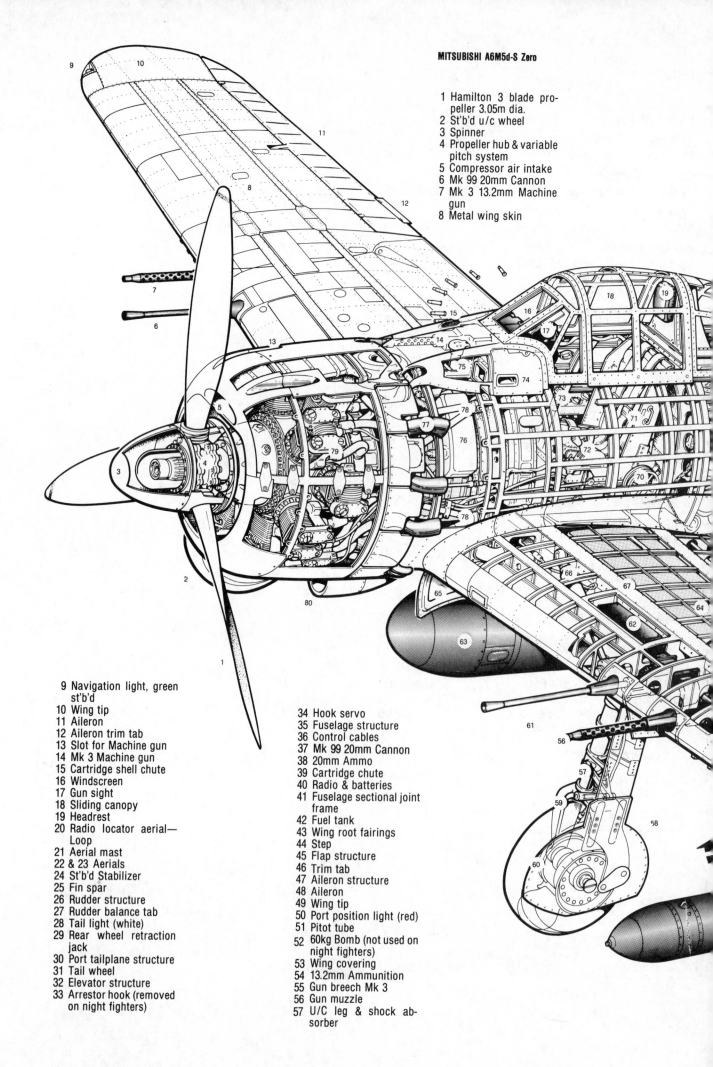

1 Hamilton 3 blade propeller 3.05m dia.
2 St'b'd u/c wheel
3 Spinner
4 Propeller hub & variable pitch system
5 Compressor air intake
6 Mk 99 20mm Cannon
7 Mk 3 13.2mm Machine gun
8 Metal wing skin

9 Navigation light, green st'b'd
10 Wing tip
11 Aileron
12 Aileron trim tab
13 Slot for Machine gun
14 Mk 3 Machine gun
15 Cartridge shell chute
16 Windscreen
17 Gun sight
18 Sliding canopy
19 Headrest
20 Radio locator aerial—Loop
21 Aerial mast
22 & 23 Aerials
24 St'b'd Stabilizer
25 Fin spar
26 Rudder structure
27 Rudder balance tab
28 Tail light (white)
29 Rear wheel retraction jack
30 Port tailplane structure
31 Tail wheel
32 Elevator structure
33 Arrestor hook (removed on night fighters)

34 Hook servo
35 Fuselage structure
36 Control cables
37 Mk 99 20mm Cannon
38 20mm Ammo
39 Cartridge chute
40 Radio & batteries
41 Fuselage sectional joint frame
42 Fuel tank
43 Wing root fairings
44 Step
45 Flap structure
46 Trim tab
47 Aileron structure
48 Aileron
49 Wing tip
50 Port position light (red)
51 Pitot tube
52 60kg Bomb (not used on night fighters)
53 Wing covering
54 13.2mm Ammunition
55 Gun breech Mk 3
56 Gun muzzle
57 U/C leg & shock absorber

58 U/C housing door
59 Fork
60 Wheel
61 Mk 99 20mm Cannon
62 20mm Ammo
63 330 litre auxiliary tank
64 Wing tank
65 U/C door
66 U/C retraction arm
67 Front spar
68 Rear spar
69 Oxygen bottles

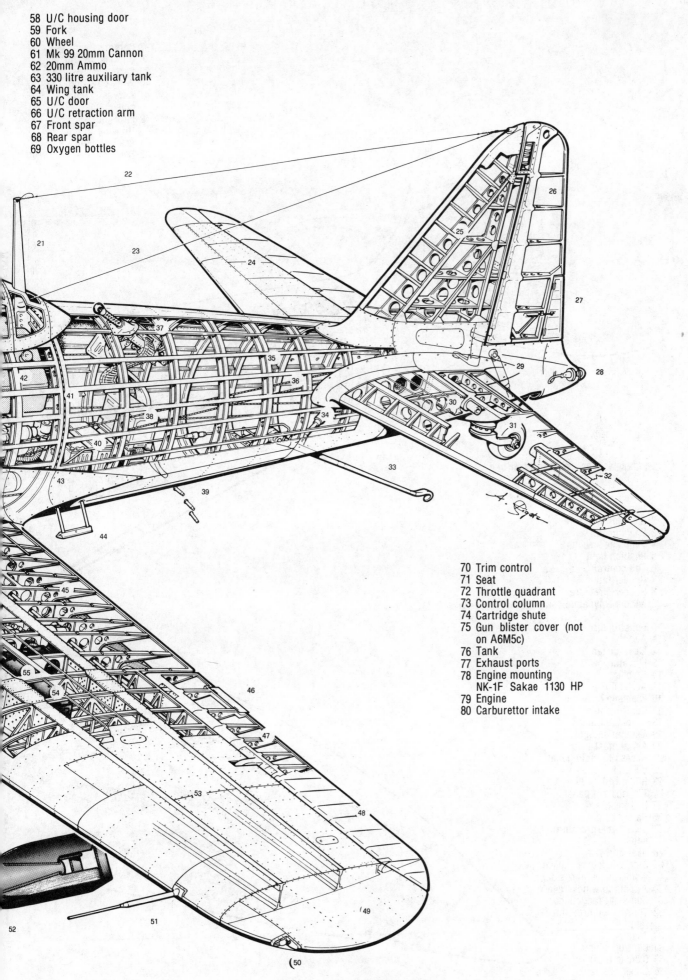

70 Trim control
71 Seat
72 Throttle quadrant
73 Control column
74 Cartridge shute
75 Gun blister cover (not
   on A6M5c)
76 Tank
77 Exhaust ports
78 Engine mounting
   NK-1F Sakae 1130 HP
79 Engine
80 Carburettor intake

5

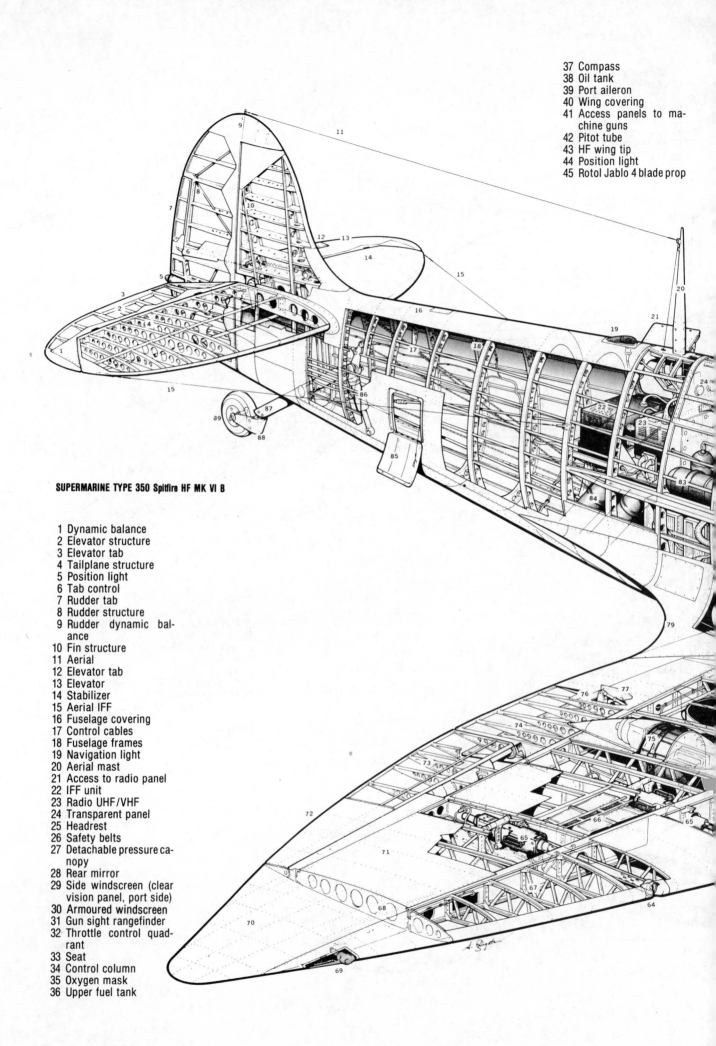

SUPERMARINE TYPE 350 Spitfire HF MK VI B

37 Compass
38 Oil tank
39 Port aileron
40 Wing covering
41 Access panels to machine guns
42 Pitot tube
43 HF wing tip
44 Position light
45 Rotol Jablo 4 blade prop

1 Dynamic balance
2 Elevator structure
3 Elevator tab
4 Tailplane structure
5 Position light
6 Tab control
7 Rudder tab
8 Rudder structure
9 Rudder dynamic balance
10 Fin structure
11 Aerial
12 Elevator tab
13 Elevator
14 Stabilizer
15 Aerial IFF
16 Fuselage covering
17 Control cables
18 Fuselage frames
19 Navigation light
20 Aerial mast
21 Access to radio panel
22 IFF unit
23 Radio UHF/VHF
24 Transparent panel
25 Headrest
26 Safety belts
27 Detachable pressure canopy
28 Rear mirror
29 Side windscreen (clear vision panel, port side)
30 Armoured windscreen
31 Gun sight rangefinder
32 Throttle control quadrant
33 Seat
34 Control column
35 Oxygen mask
36 Upper fuel tank

46 Spar
47 Gun
48 20mm (muzzle brake) Hispano Cannon
49 Spinner
50 Variable pitch mechanism
51 Propeller hub
52 Glycol tank
53 Merlin 47 1415 HP Engine
54 Exhaust ports
55 Engine mounting
56 U/C housing door
57 Wheel
58 Leading edge
59 U/C leg
60 U/C cover
61 Hispano Cannon 20mm
62 Wheel
63 Tyre
64 Guns
65 Browning 7.7mm

66 Ammunition boxes
67 Structure
68 Front spar
69 Position light
70 HF wingtip
71 Covering
72 Aileron
73 Structure
74 Flap
75 70mm gun blister
76 Flap horn
77 Opening panel
78 Wheel well
79 Wing root fairings
80 Oxygen bottles plant
81 U/C control lever
82 Rudder pedals bar
83 Oxygen bottles
84 Flare chute
85 Fuselage access panel
86 Tail wheel shock absorber
87 Tail wheel leg
88 Tail wheel fork
89 Tail wheel

Supermarine Type 300 Spitfire 1A Data

Power plant: Rolls Royce Merlin III 12 cylinder V, liquid cooled 1030 HP. 3 blade propeller, metal, 2 position.
2 tanks, 218 litres and 168 litres.
Dimensions: wing span 11.22m; length 9.12m, height 3.45; surface 22.50mq.
Performance: Maximum speed 580 kmh at 5800m.
Initial climb speed 12.6m/sec; climb to 6000m 9 mins 24 secs.
Ceiling 10,300m; range 915km;
Armament 8 Browning 7.7 machine guns with 300 rounds each.
(MK VI aircraft for high altitude escort illustrated)

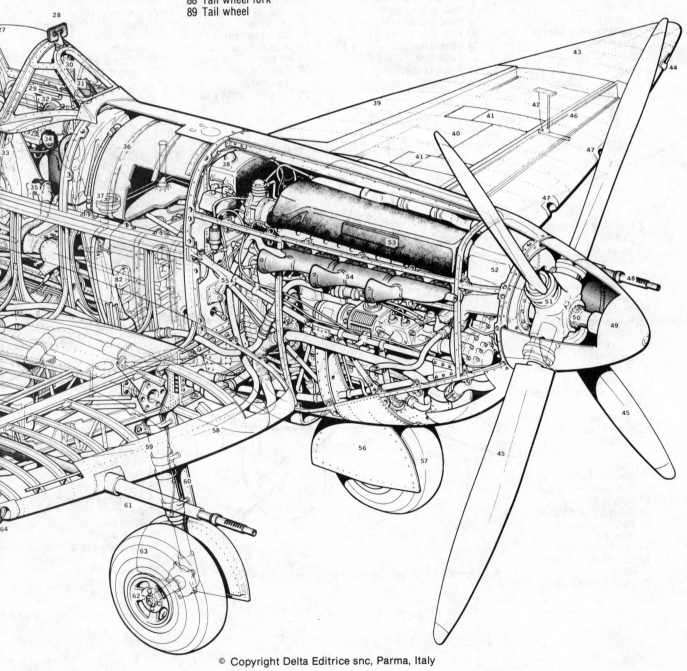

MACCHI C 202 AS/CB Folgore SERIES IX

Macchi C202

Engine: Alfa Romeo RA 1000 R.C. 41 Monsone (Daimler Benz DB 601Aa under licence 12 Cyl. inverted V, liquid cooled 1175hp (take off) 1030hp at 4100m. Propeller: Piaggio metal 3 bladed variable pitch, 3.05
Fuel: 430 internal, 300 litres external.
Dimensions: Span 10.58m, length 8.85m, height 3.3m, surface 16.08sq.m.
Performance: Max speed 599kmh at 5600m. Climb to 1000m 59 sec, 2000m 1.20 sec, 3000 2.28 secs, 4000 3.32 sec, 5000 4 min 4 sec, 6000 5 min 55 sec. Ceiling 11500m. Range 765km.
Armament: 2 machine guns Breda Safat 12.7mm 500 rounds firing through the propeller disc plus 2 wing mounted 7.7mm Breda Safat machine guns and 2 bombs 50,100 or 160kg.

1 Piaggio P 1001 3 blade metal propeller
2 Propeller shaft
3 Spinner
4 Variable pitch (Worm-gear)
5 Propeller hub

29 Armoured windscreen
30 Gun sight rangefinder
31 Rear armour plate
32 Head armour plate
33 Rear view cutaway
34 Petrol filler cap
35 Aerial mast
36 Aerial connector

37 Aerial
38 Antiroll structure
39 80 litres tank
40 Radio equipment B.30
41 Cockpit fairings
42 Panel for radio inspection
43 Fuselage structure and rudder cable
44 Access panel
45 Stabilizer
46 Elevator
47 Fin fairing
48 Fin structure
49 Rudder balance horn
50 Rudder structure
51 Rudder
52 Tail cone
53 Navigation light (white)
54 Elevator structure
55 Tailplane structure
56 Tail wheel
57 Tail wheel fairing
58 Controls levers and lifting point
59 Incidence control mechanism
60 Tailwheel brake cable

61 Restraint rod
62 Tailwheel pivot
63 Shock ram
64 Casting
65 Tail wheel stanchion
66 Fork
67 Turnbuckles
68 Elevator control rod
69 Compressed air bottle
70 Fire extinguisher
71 Pressure accumulator
72 Oxygen
73 Step
74 Wing root fairings
75 Spar joint
76 Rear spar
77 Trailing edge structure
78 Trailing edge
79 Optical signal U/C position
80 U/C axle
81 Breda SAFAT 7.7mm machine gun (500 rounds)
82 7.7mm ammunition
83 Leading edge structure

6 Mechanism variable pitch
7 Air scoops (2)
8 Right wing
9 Electric cable
10 Aileron pushrods
11 Navigation light, green
12 Aileron
13 Flap drive shafts
14 Alfa-Romeo R.A.1000 R.C.41.1 Monsone 1175 Hp engine
15 Antivibration engine mounting
16 Machine gun channels
17 Zenith compressor
18 Water tank
19 Machine gun barrel
20 Oil tank
21 Secondary optical gun sight
22 Breda SAFAT MC 12.7mm machine gun
23 Battery (2)
24 Air scoop and battery
25 Port machine gun—breech
26 Ammunition feed
27 Secondary optical gun sight
28 Instrument panel

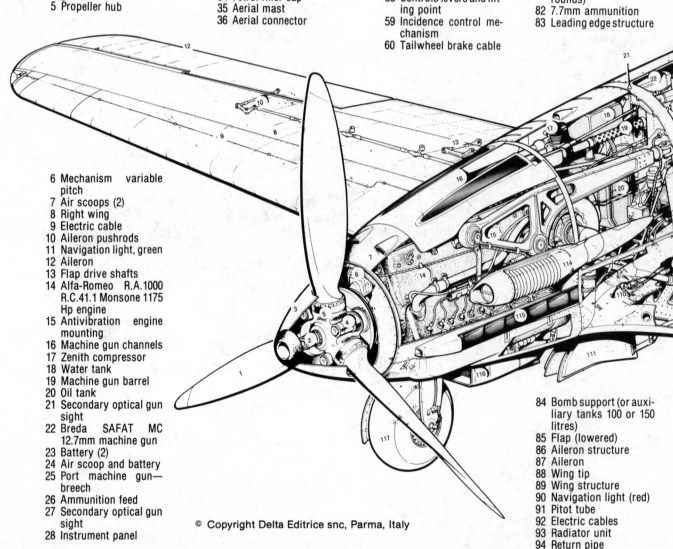

© Copyright Delta Editrice snc, Parma, Italy

84 Bomb support (or auxiliary tanks 100 or 150 litres)
85 Flap (lowered)
86 Aileron structure
87 Aileron
88 Wing tip
89 Wing structure
90 Navigation light (red)
91 Pitot tube
92 Electric cables
93 Radiator unit
94 Return pipe

8

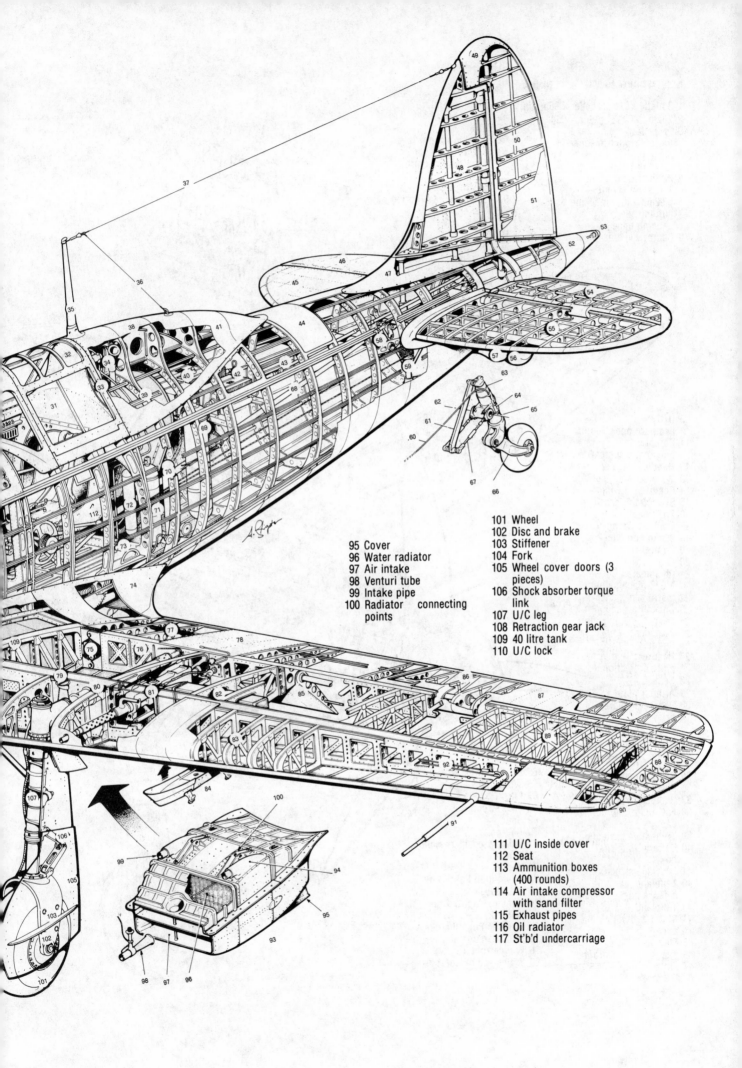

95 Cover
96 Water radiator
97 Air intake
98 Venturi tube
99 Intake pipe
100 Radiator connecting
points

101 Wheel
102 Disc and brake
103 Stiffener
104 Fork
105 Wheel cover doors (3
pieces)
106 Shock absorber torque
link
107 U/C leg
108 Retraction gear jack
109 40 litre tank
110 U/C lock

111 U/C inside cover
112 Seat
113 Ammunition boxes
(400 rounds)
114 Air intake compressor
with sand filter
115 Exhaust pipes
116 Oil radiator
117 St'b'd undercarriage

1 3 blade VDM propeller 2.96m dia.
2 20mm MG/151 gun muzzle
3 Propeller hub and variable pitch mechanism
4 Oil tank
5 Daimler Benz DB 603E-1 1350 Hp engine
6 7.92mm MG17 machine gun muzzle
7 Leading edge
8 Compressed air pipes

49 Rudder structure
50 Rear light (white)
51 Tab
52 Elevator structure
53 Balance
54 Stabilizer structure
55 Rudder horn
56 Tailwheel well
57 Tailwheel leg spring blockage
58 Fork
59 Tailwheel
60 Compressed air tanks for fuselage guns
61 First aid locker
62 Telecompass

9 U/C Well
10 Leading edge structure
11 Compressed air tanks, pneumatic system
12 Handley-Page slat
13 Wing covering surface
14 Removable wing tip
15 St'b'd light, green
16 Frise aileron
17 Trim tab, set on ground
18 20mm gun duct
19 Control rods
20 Flap
21 Rheinmetall Borsig MG17 machine gun
22 Instrument panel
23 Cockpit air scoop
24 Revi C12/D gunsight
25 Armoured windscreen
26 Canopy
27 Headrest and armour plate protection
28 Seat
29 Armour plate
30 Rear transparent panels
31 Aerial mast
32 Handle
33 Aerial
34 Methylated spirit tank
35 Oxygen bottles
36 FuG 7a radio
37 Radioelectric system
38 FuG units and control cables
39 Trim cable protection
40 Battery and first aid box
41 Fuselage structure
42 Tailplane variable incidence angle system
43 Tailplane
44 Static & dynamic balance
45 Elevator
46 Tab to be set on ground
47 Fin structure
48 Balance

63 Whip aerial
64 Flap mechanism
65 Flaps depressed
66 Wing root fairings
67 Flap
68 Flap structure
69 Spar
70 Aileron
71 Balance, counterweight
72 Tab
73 Wingtip
74 Navigation light (red)
75 Pitot tube
76 Handley-Page slat control link
77 Handley-Page link (2)
78 Handley-Page slat
79 Wing structure
80 Water and glycol radiator

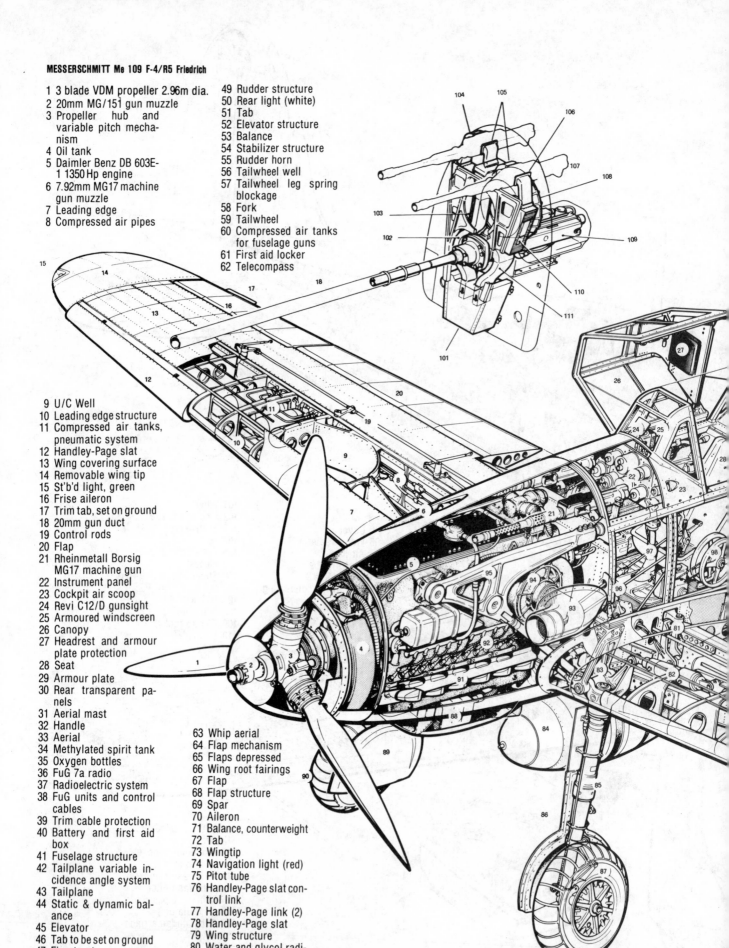

10

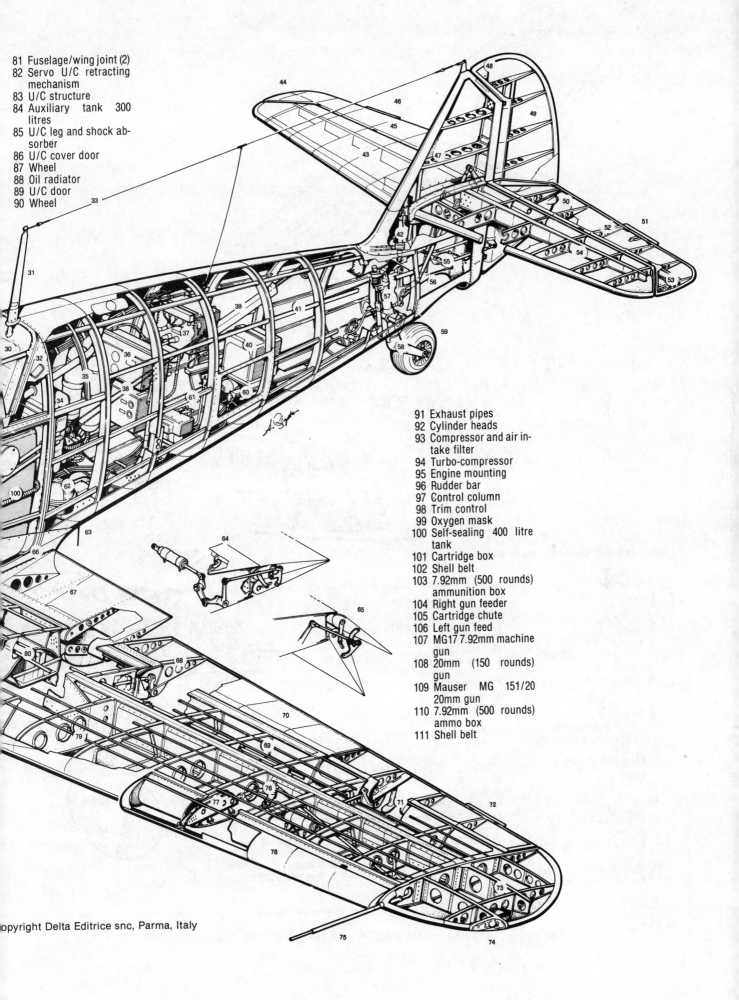

81 Fuselage/wing joint (2)
82 Servo U/C retracting mechanism
83 U/C structure
84 Auxiliary tank 300 litres
85 U/C leg and shock absorber
86 U/C cover door
87 Wheel
88 Oil radiator
89 U/C door
90 Wheel

91 Exhaust pipes
92 Cylinder heads
93 Compressor and air intake filter
94 Turbo-compressor
95 Engine mounting
96 Rudder bar
97 Control column
98 Trim control
99 Oxygen mask
100 Self-sealing 400 litre tank
101 Cartridge box
102 Shell belt
103 7.92mm (500 rounds) ammunition box
104 Right gun feeder
105 Cartridge chute
106 Left gun feed
107 MG17 7.92mm machine gun
108 20mm (150 rounds) gun
109 Mauser MG 151/20 20mm gun
110 7.92mm (500 rounds) ammo box
111 Shell belt

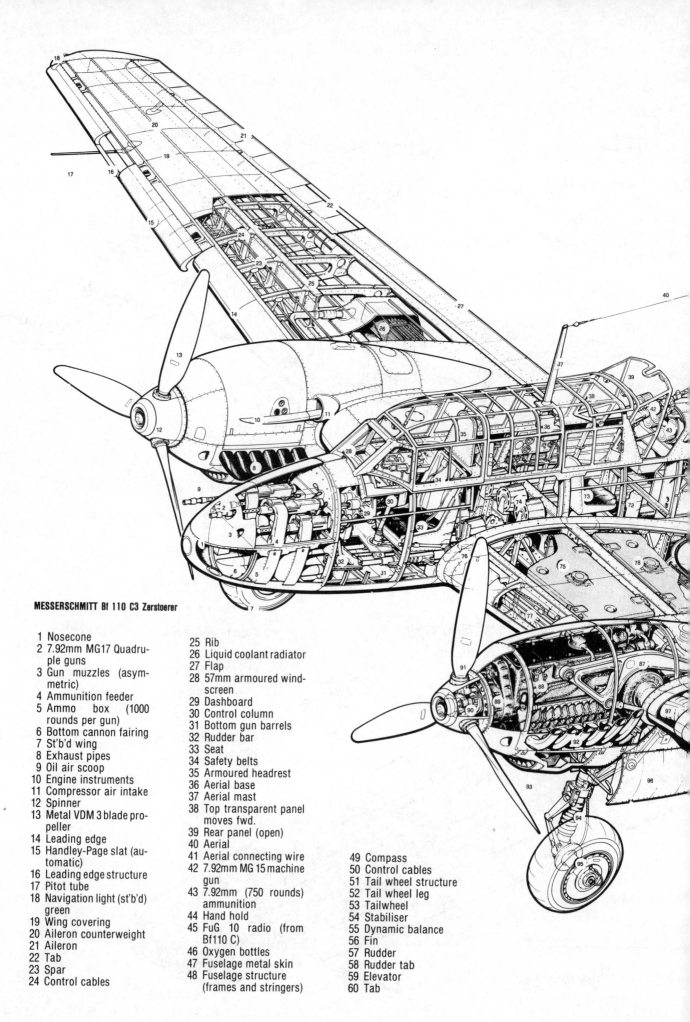

MESSERSCHMITT Bf 110 C3 Zerstoerer

1 Nosecone
2 7.92mm MG17 Quadruple guns
3 Gun muzzles (asymmetric)
4 Ammunition feeder
5 Ammo box (1000 rounds per gun)
6 Bottom cannon fairing
7 St'b'd wing
8 Exhaust pipes
9 Oil air scoop
10 Engine instruments
11 Compressor air intake
12 Spinner
13 Metal VDM 3 blade propeller
14 Leading edge
15 Handley-Page slat (automatic)
16 Leading edge structure
17 Pitot tube
18 Navigation light (st'b'd) green
19 Wing covering
20 Aileron counterweight
21 Aileron
22 Tab
23 Spar
24 Control cables

25 Rib
26 Liquid coolant radiator
27 Flap
28 57mm armoured windscreen
29 Dashboard
30 Control column
31 Bottom gun barrels
32 Rudder bar
33 Seat
34 Safety belts
35 Armoured headrest
36 Aerial base
37 Aerial mast
38 Top transparent panel moves fwd.
39 Rear panel (open)
40 Aerial
41 Aerial connecting wire
42 7.92mm MG 15 machine gun
43 7.92mm (750 rounds) ammunition
44 Hand hold
45 FuG 10 radio (from Bf110 C)
46 Oxygen bottles
47 Fuselage metal skin
48 Fuselage structure (frames and stringers)

49 Compass
50 Control cables
51 Tail wheel structure
52 Tail wheel leg
53 Tailwheel
54 Stabiliser
55 Dynamic balance
56 Fin
57 Rudder
58 Rudder tab
59 Elevator
60 Tab

61 Elevator structure
62 Tab
63 Stabilizer structure
64 Fin structure
65 Rudder structure
66 Tab
67 Aerial synthesizer
68 Aerial
69 Battery

70 First aid box
71 Transformer
72 Fire extinguisher
73 Observer/gunner's seat
74 20mm (180 rounds) ammo
75 Petrol tank
76 20mm MG-FF guns (2)
77 Leading edge structure and cables

78 Petrol tank
79 Flap rib
80 Radio loop
81 Wing root fairings
82 Retractable step ladder
83 Tubular spar
84 Flap
85 Flap control
86 Oil tank
87 Engine mounting

88 Daimler BenzDB 601A1 12 Cyl. Vol, liquid cooled 1050–1100hp
89 Reduction gear
90 Hub and variable pitch mechanism
91 3 blades metal prop VDM
92 Exhaust pipes
93 Oil radiator air intake
94 Shock absorber with covering protection
95 Wheel, tyre and brake
96 U/C door
97 Compressor air duct
98 Compressor air intake
99 Landing lights

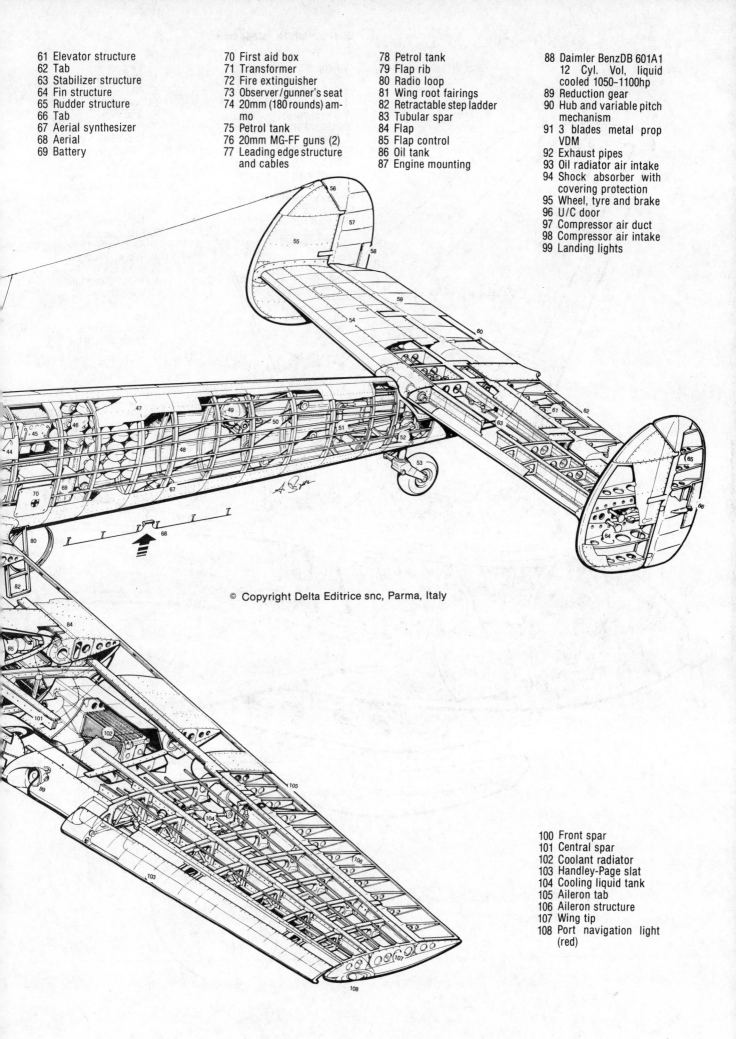

100 Front spar
101 Central spar
102 Coolant radiator
103 Handley-Page slat
104 Cooling liquid tank
105 Aileron tab
106 Aileron structure
107 Wing tip
108 Port navigation light (red)

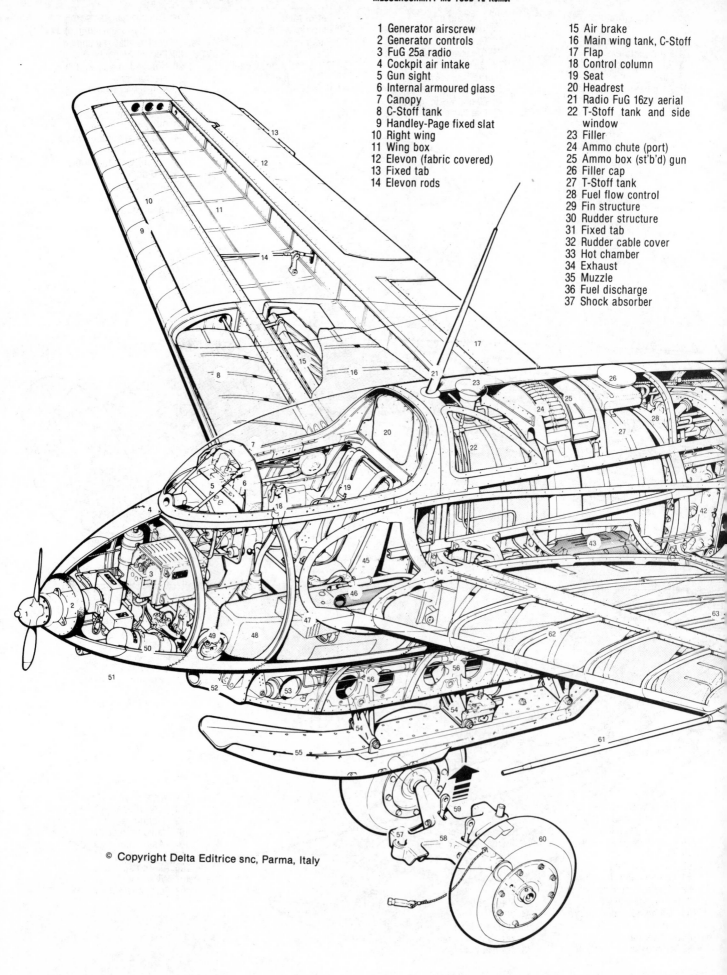

MESSERSCHMITT Me 163B-1a Komet

1 Generator airscrew
2 Generator controls
3 FuG 25a radio
4 Cockpit air intake
5 Gun sight
6 Internal armoured glass
7 Canopy
8 C-Stoff tank
9 Handley-Page fixed slat
10 Right wing
11 Wing box
12 Elevon (fabric covered)
13 Fixed tab
14 Elevon rods

15 Air brake
16 Main wing tank, C-Stoff
17 Flap
18 Control column
19 Seat
20 Headrest
21 Radio FuG 16zy aerial
22 T-Stoff tank and side window
23 Filler
24 Ammo chute (port)
25 Ammo box (st'b'd) gun
26 Filler cap
27 T-Stoff tank
28 Fuel flow control
29 Fin structure
30 Rudder structure
31 Fixed tab
32 Rudder cable cover
33 Hot chamber
34 Exhaust
35 Muzzle
36 Fuel discharge
37 Shock absorber

14

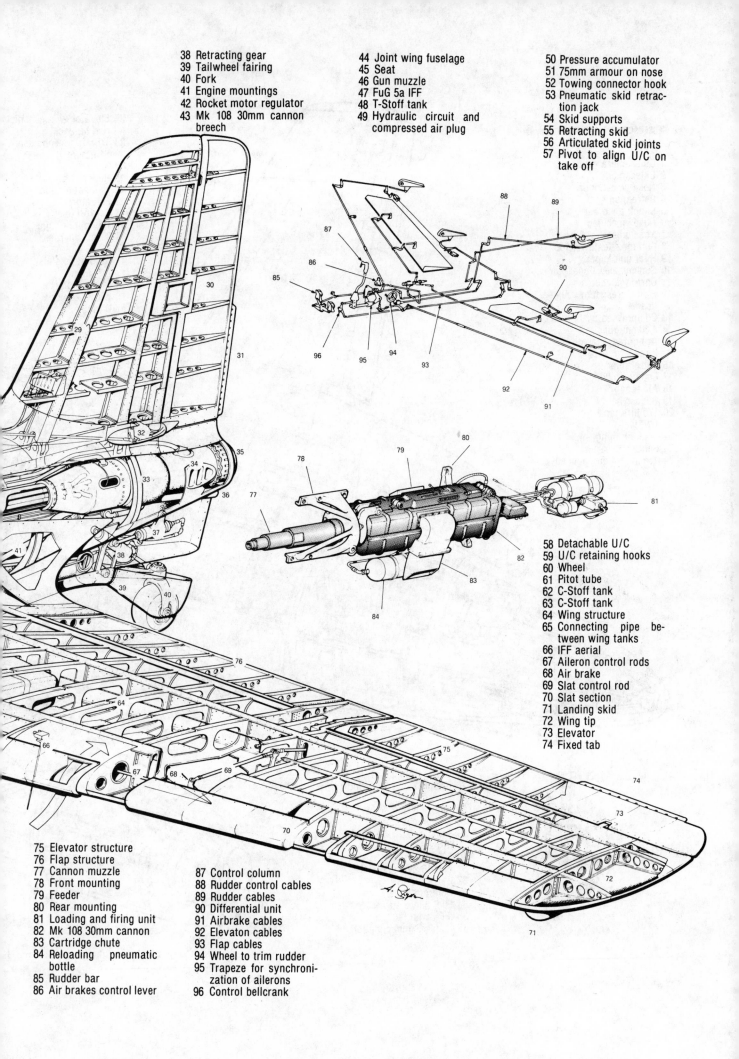

38 Retracting gear
39 Tailwheel fairing
40 Fork
41 Engine mountings
42 Rocket motor regulator
43 Mk 108 30mm cannon breech

44 Joint wing fuselage
45 Seat
46 Gun muzzle
47 FuG 5a IFF
48 T-Stoff tank
49 Hydraulic circuit and compressed air plug

50 Pressure accumulator
51 75mm armour on nose
52 Towing connector hook
53 Pneumatic skid retraction jack
54 Skid supports
55 Retracting skid
56 Articulated skid joints
57 Pivot to align U/C on take off

58 Detachable U/C
59 U/C retaining hooks
60 Wheel
61 Pitot tube
62 C-Stoff tank
63 C-Stoff tank
64 Wing structure
65 Connecting pipe between wing tanks
66 IFF aerial
67 Aileron control rods
68 Air brake
69 Slat control rod
70 Slat section
71 Landing skid
72 Wing tip
73 Elevator
74 Fixed tab

75 Elevator structure
76 Flap structure
77 Cannon muzzle
78 Front mounting
79 Feeder
80 Rear mounting
81 Loading and firing unit
82 Mk 108 30mm cannon
83 Cartridge chute
84 Reloading pneumatic bottle
85 Rudder bar
86 Air brakes control lever

87 Control column
88 Rudder control cables
89 Rudder cables
90 Differential unit
91 Airbrake cables
92 Elevaton cables
93 Flap cables
94 Wheel to trim rudder
95 Trapeze for synchronization of ailerons
96 Control bellcrank

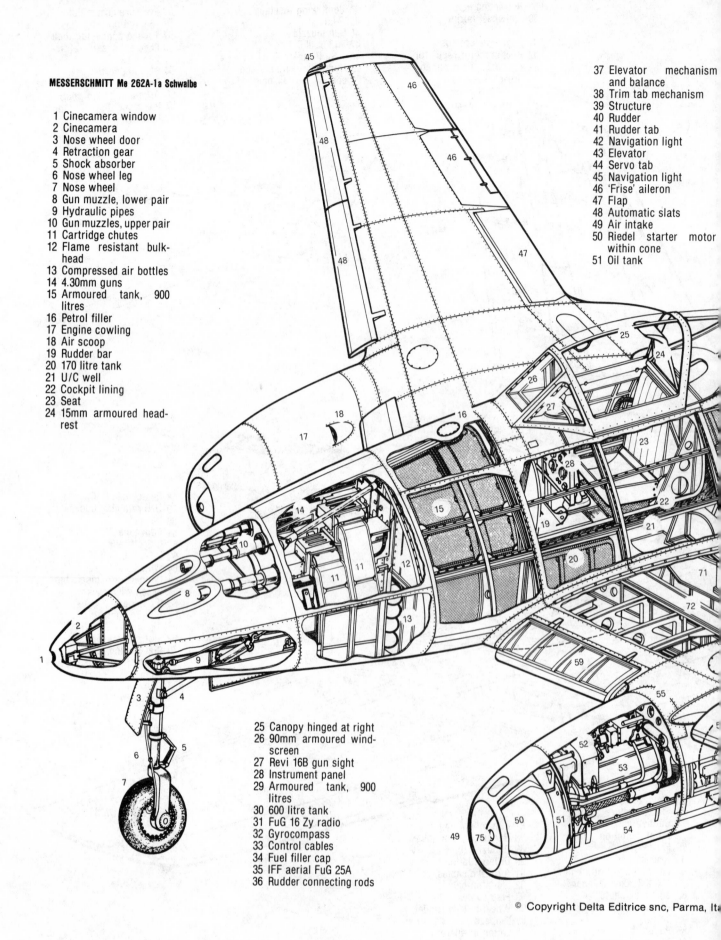

MESSERSCHMITT Me 262A-1a Schwalbe

1 Cinecamera window
2 Cinecamera
3 Nose wheel door
4 Retraction gear
5 Shock absorber
6 Nose wheel leg
7 Nose wheel
8 Gun muzzle, lower pair
9 Hydraulic pipes
10 Gun muzzles, upper pair
11 Cartridge chutes
12 Flame resistant bulk-head
13 Compressed air bottles
14 4.30mm guns
15 Armoured tank, 900 litres
16 Petrol filler
17 Engine cowling
18 Air scoop
19 Rudder bar
20 170 litre tank
21 U/C well
22 Cockpit lining
23 Seat
24 15mm armoured head-rest

25 Canopy hinged at right
26 90mm armoured wind-screen
27 Revi 16B gun sight
28 Instrument panel
29 Armoured tank, 900 litres
30 600 litre tank
31 FuG 16 Zy radio
32 Gyrocompass
33 Control cables
34 Fuel filler cap
35 IFF aerial FuG 25A
36 Rudder connecting rods

37 Elevator mechanism and balance
38 Trim tab mechanism
39 Structure
40 Rudder
41 Rudder tab
42 Navigation light
43 Elevator
44 Servo tab
45 Navigation light
46 'Frise' aileron
47 Flap
48 Automatic slats
49 Air intake
50 Riedel starter motor within cone
51 Oil tank

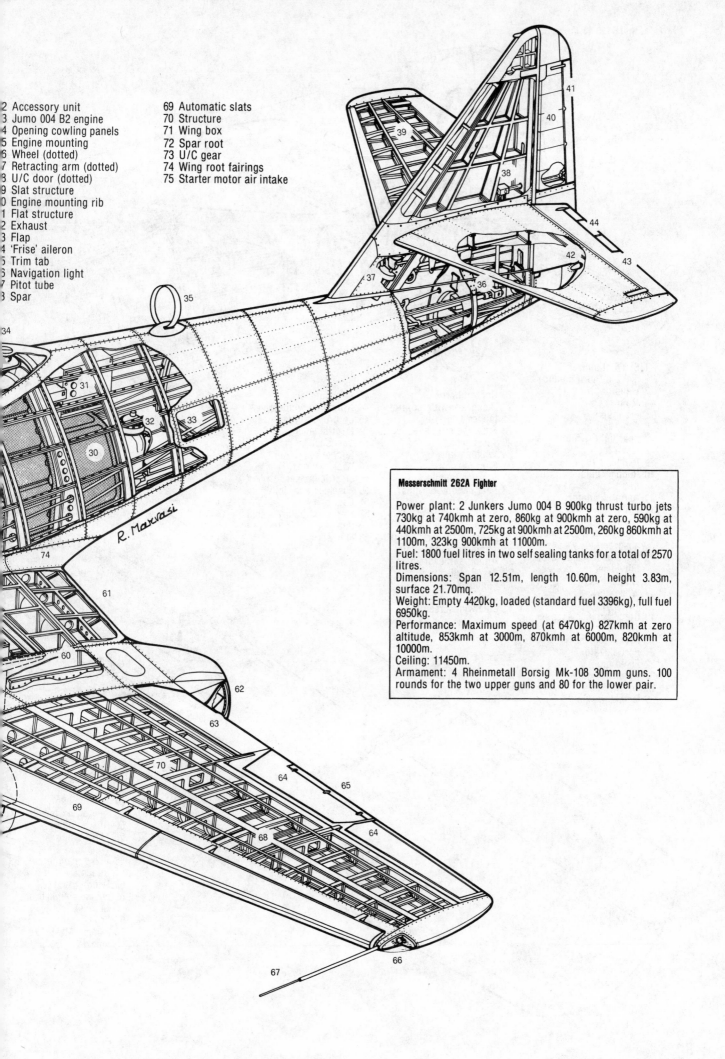

2 Accessory unit
3 Jumo 004 B2 engine
4 Opening cowling panels
5 Engine mounting
6 Wheel (dotted)
7 Retracting arm (dotted)
8 U/C door (dotted)
9 Slat structure
0 Engine mounting rib
1 Flat structure
2 Exhaust
3 Flap
4 'Frise' aileron
5 Trim tab
6 Navigation light
7 Pitot tube
8 Spar

69 Automatic slats
70 Structure
71 Wing box
72 Spar root
73 U/C gear
74 Wing root fairings
75 Starter motor air intake

R. Mavrasi

Messerschmitt 262A Fighter

Power plant: 2 Junkers Jumo 004 B 900kg thrust turbo jets 730kg at 740kmh at zero, 860kg at 900kmh at zero, 590kg at 440kmh at 2500m, 725kg at 900kmh at 2500m, 260kg 860kmh at 1100m, 323kg 900kmh at 11000m.
Fuel: 1800 fuel litres in two self sealing tanks for a total of 2570 litres.
Dimensions: Span 12.51m, length 10.60m, height 3.83m, surface 21.70mq.
Weight: Empty 4420kg, loaded (standard fuel 3396kg), full fuel 6950kg.
Performance: Maximum speed (at 6470kg) 827kmh at zero altitude, 853kmh at 3000m, 870kmh at 6000m, 820kmh at 10000m.
Ceiling: 11450m.
Armament: 4 Rheinmetall Borsig Mk-108 30mm guns. 100 rounds for the two upper guns and 80 for the lower pair.

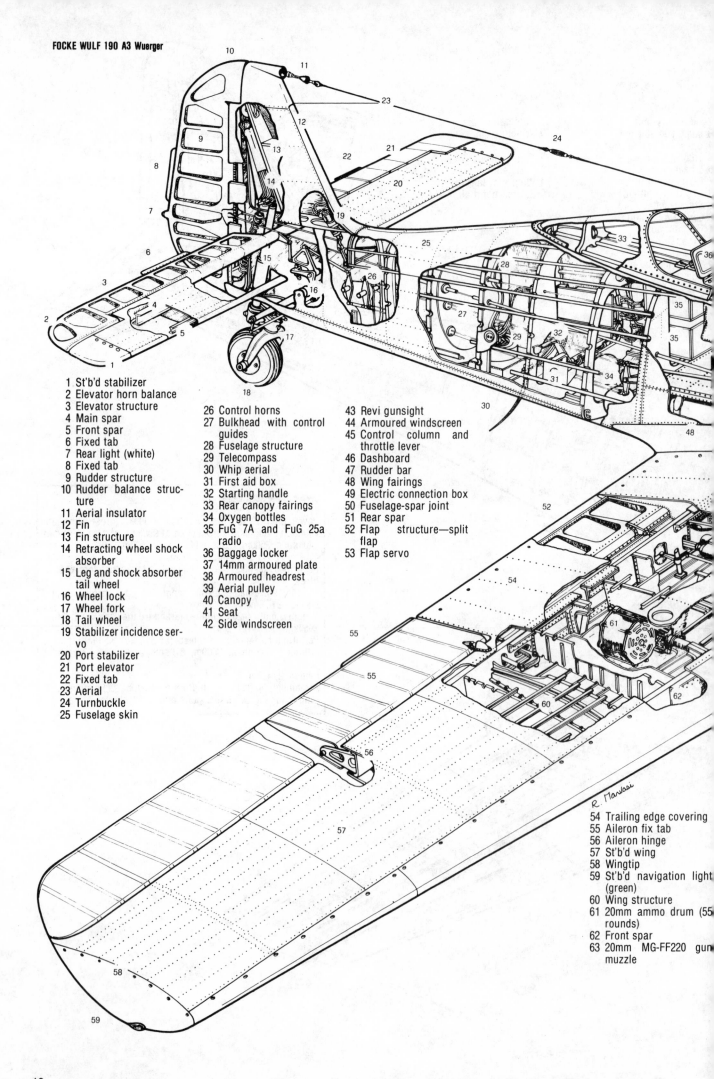

1 St'b'd stabilizer
2 Elevator horn balance
3 Elevator structure
4 Main spar
5 Front spar
6 Fixed tab
7 Rear light (white)
8 Fixed tab
9 Rudder structure
10 Rudder balance structure
11 Aerial insulator
12 Fin
13 Fin structure
14 Retracting wheel shock absorber
15 Leg and shock absorber tail wheel
16 Wheel lock
17 Wheel fork
18 Tail wheel
19 Stabilizer incidence servo
20 Port stabilizer
21 Port elevator
22 Fixed tab
23 Aerial
24 Turnbuckle
25 Fuselage skin

26 Control horns
27 Bulkhead with control guides
28 Fuselage structure
29 Telecompass
30 Whip aerial
31 First aid box
32 Starting handle
33 Rear canopy fairings
34 Oxygen bottles
35 FuG 7A and FuG 25a radio
36 Baggage locker
37 14mm armoured plate
38 Armoured headrest
39 Aerial pulley
40 Canopy
41 Seat
42 Side windscreen

43 Revi gunsight
44 Armoured windscreen
45 Control column and throttle lever
46 Dashboard
47 Rudder bar
48 Wing fairings
49 Electric connection box
50 Fuselage-spar joint
51 Rear spar
52 Flap structure—split flap
53 Flap servo

54 Trailing edge covering
55 Aileron fix tab
56 Aileron hinge
57 St'b'd wing
58 Wingtip
59 St'b'd navigation light (green)
60 Wing structure
61 20mm ammo drum (55 rounds)
62 Front spar
63 20mm MG-FF220 gun muzzle

R. Marvasi

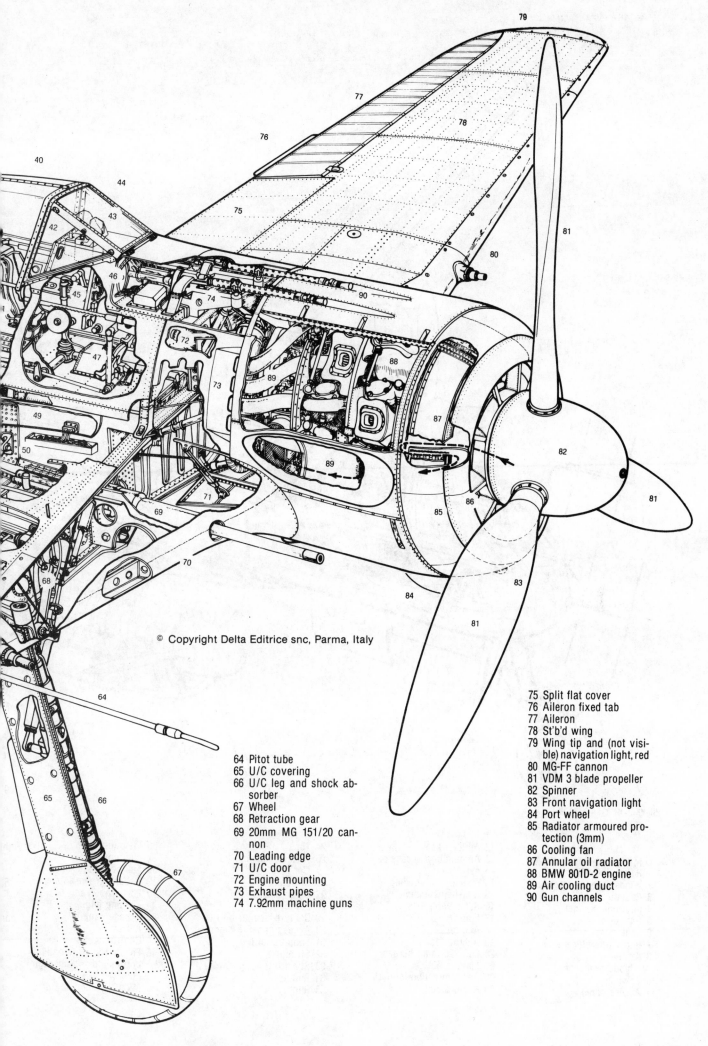

© Copyright Delta Editrice snc, Parma, Italy

64 Pitot tube
65 U/C covering
66 U/C leg and shock absorber
67 Wheel
68 Retraction gear
69 20mm MG 151/20 cannon
70 Leading edge
71 U/C door
72 Engine mounting
73 Exhaust pipes
74 7.92mm machine guns

75 Split flat cover
76 Aileron fixed tab
77 Aileron
78 St'b'd wing
79 Wing tip and (not visible) navigation light, red
80 MG-FF cannon
81 VDM 3 blade propeller
82 Spinner
83 Front navigation light
84 Port wheel
85 Radiator armoured protection (3mm)
86 Cooling fan
87 Annular oil radiator
88 BMW 801D-2 engine
89 Air cooling duct
90 Gun channels

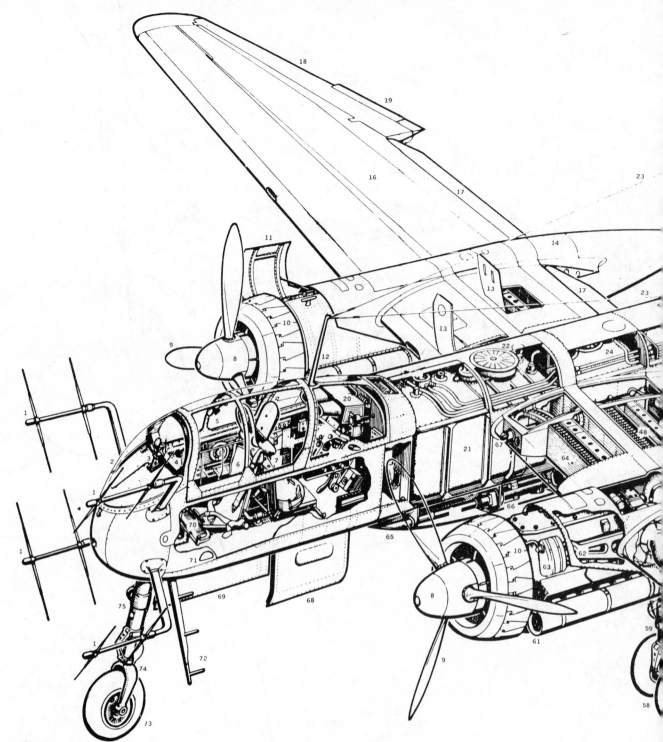

HEINKEL He 219A-7/R4 Uhu

1 Aerial, Hirschgeweih, for Lichtenstein SN-2 Radar FuG 220
2 Windscreen unprotected
3 Revi gunsight
4 Instrument panel
5 Canopy
6 Seat
7 Radar operator's seat
8 Spinner
9 3 blade propeller
10 Cowling
11 Access panel

12 Aerial mast
13 Ammunition access panel
14 Engine rear cowling
15 Nacelle extension
16 St'b'd wing
17 Flap
18 Aileron
19 Aileron tab
20 FuG 220 radar screen
21 Main tank
22 Radio direction loop
23 Radio aerial

24 Tank
25 "Schraege musik" muzzles
26 Structure
27 Radio electric winch
28 Dinghy
29 Compressed air bottle
30 Access panel to dinghy
31 Loop aerial IFF
32 Structure
33 St'b'd fin
34 Rudder
35 Rudder tab

36 Elevator
37 Elevator tab
38 Tab control
39 Radar warning antennae
40 Port stabilizer
41 Leading edge
42 Access panel
43 Aerial
44 Control cables
45 Pneumatic reloading bottles for "Schraege musik"
46 Mk 108 30mm cannons

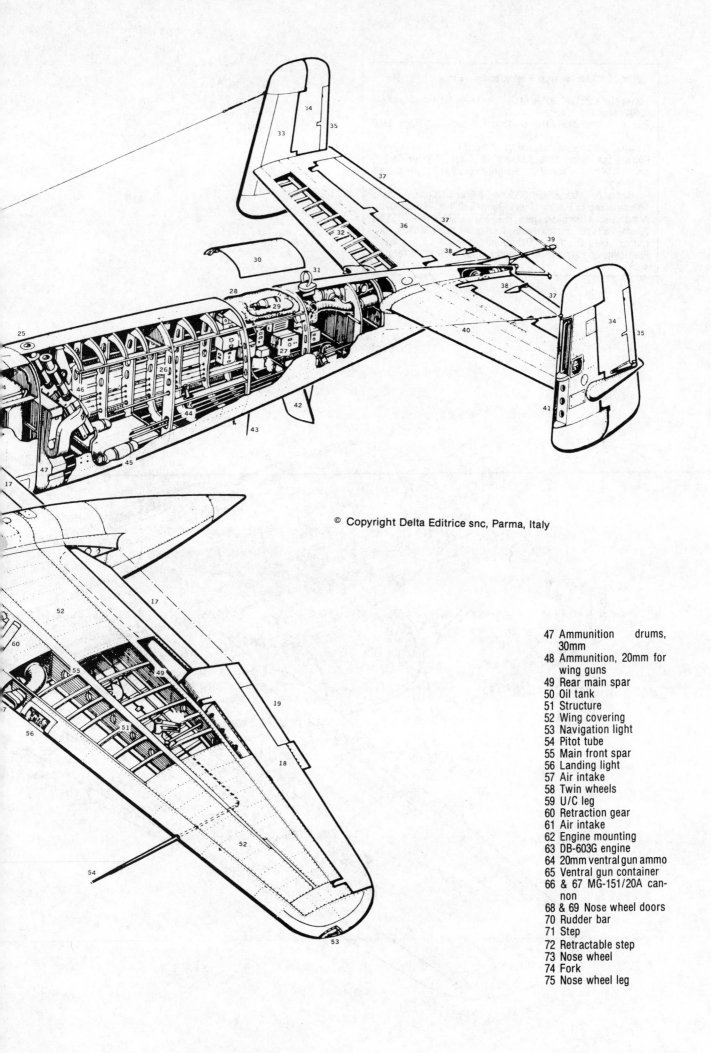

47 Ammunition drums, 30mm
48 Ammunition, 20mm for wing guns
49 Rear main spar
50 Oil tank
51 Structure
52 Wing covering
53 Navigation light
54 Pitot tube
55 Main front spar
56 Landing light
57 Air intake
58 Twin wheels
59 U/C leg
60 Retraction gear
61 Air intake
62 Engine mounting
63 DB-603G engine
64 20mm ventral gun ammo
65 Ventral gun container
66 & 67 MG-151/20A cannon
68 & 69 Nose wheel doors
70 Rudder bar
71 Step
72 Retractable step
73 Nose wheel
74 Fork
75 Nose wheel leg

Dornier DO 217J-2: Interceptor & fighter/bomber—3 crew

Power plant: 2 BMW 801ML 14 Cyl. air cooled 1580hp on take off (2400 revs) and 1380hp at 4600m.
Fuel capacity: 2950 litres plus internal auxiliary tank 1160 litres.
3 bladed props wooden Schwarz or metal VDM variable pitch.
Dimensions: Span 19mm, length 18.20 (or 17.91 or 18.84), height 4.98m, surface 57.0m, weight empty 9340kg, at take off 13.165kg.
Performance: Max speed 528kmh, 490 at 5500mm, landing 180km, climb to 6000m 17 min. Range 2300km, max 3840km.
Armament: 4 Oerlikon guns MG-FFM or Mauser MG151-20 20mm, 250–350 rounds each, 4 machine guns MG131 1000 rounds, plus 2 on top 500 rounds, ventral 1000 rounds. Possibility to carry up to 8 bombs SC50X 50kg to a total of 400kg.

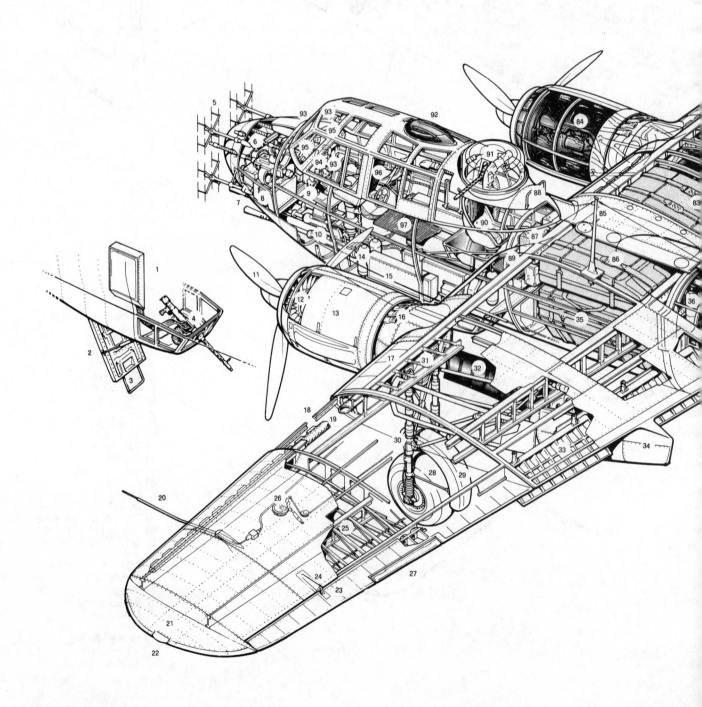

DORNIER 217J-2

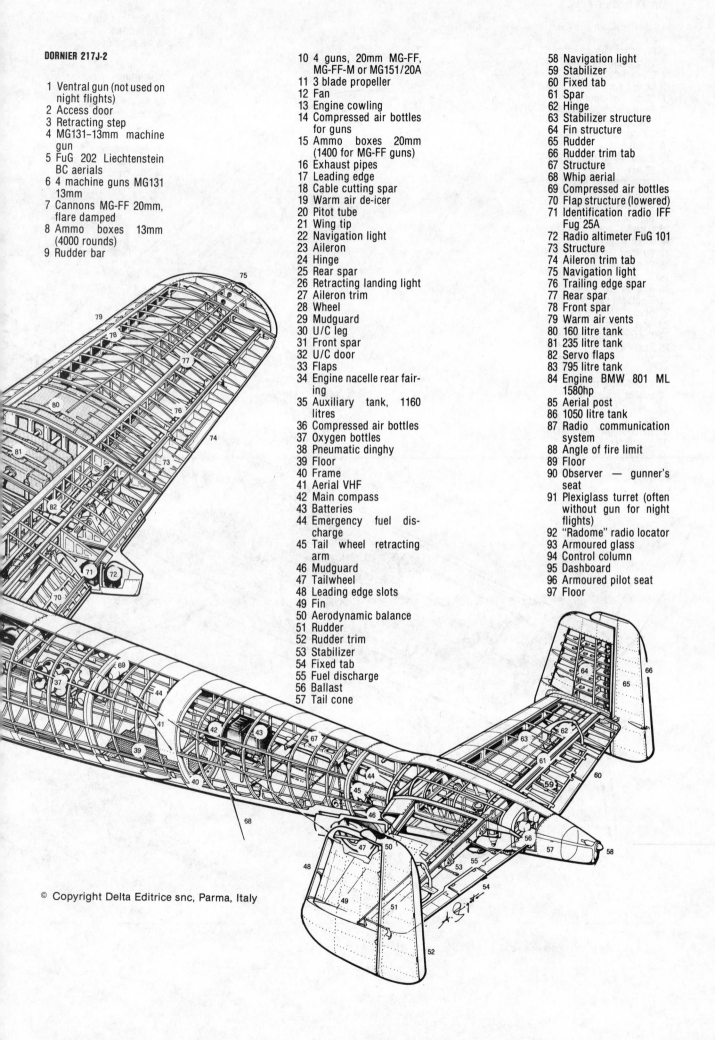

1 Ventral gun (not used on night flights)
2 Access door
3 Retracting step
4 MG131–13mm machine gun
5 FuG 202 Liechtenstein BC aerials
6 4 machine guns MG131 13mm
7 Cannons MG-FF 20mm, flare damped
8 Ammo boxes 13mm (4000 rounds)
9 Rudder bar

10 4 guns, 20mm MG-FF, MG-FF-M or MG151/20A
11 3 blade propeller
12 Fan
13 Engine cowling
14 Compressed air bottles for guns
15 Ammo boxes 20mm (1400 for MG-FF guns)
16 Exhaust pipes
17 Leading edge
18 Cable cutting spar
19 Warm air de-icer
20 Pitot tube
21 Wing tip
22 Navigation light
23 Aileron
24 Hinge
25 Rear spar
26 Retracting landing light
27 Aileron trim
28 Wheel
29 Mudguard
30 U/C leg
31 Front spar
32 U/C door
33 Flaps
34 Engine nacelle rear fairing
35 Auxiliary tank, 1160 litres
36 Compressed air bottles
37 Oxygen bottles
38 Pneumatic dinghy
39 Floor
40 Frame
41 Aerial VHF
42 Main compass
43 Batteries
44 Emergency fuel discharge
45 Tail wheel retracting arm
46 Mudguard
47 Tailwheel
48 Leading edge slots
49 Fin
50 Aerodynamic balance
51 Rudder
52 Rudder trim
53 Stabilizer
54 Fixed tab
55 Fuel discharge
56 Ballast
57 Tail cone

58 Navigation light
59 Stabilizer
60 Fixed tab
61 Spar
62 Hinge
63 Stabilizer structure
64 Fin structure
65 Rudder
66 Rudder trim tab
67 Structure
68 Whip aerial
69 Compressed air bottles
70 Flap structure (lowered)
71 Identification radio IFF Fug 25A
72 Radio altimeter FuG 101
73 Structure
74 Aileron trim tab
75 Navigation light
76 Trailing edge spar
77 Rear spar
78 Front spar
79 Warm air vents
80 160 litre tank
81 235 litre tank
82 Servo flaps
83 795 litre tank
84 Engine BMW 801 ML 1580hp
85 Aerial post
86 1050 litre tank
87 Radio communication system
88 Angle of fire limit
89 Floor
90 Observer — gunner's seat
91 Plexiglass turret (often without gun for night flights)
92 "Radome" radio locator
93 Armoured glass
94 Control column
95 Dashboard
96 Armoured pilot seat
97 Floor

DORNIER Do.335 V14 Pfeil

1 Mk 103 30mm gun muzzle
2 Propeller hub
3 VDM propeller blade
4 Oil radiator
5 Cowl flaps
6 20mm gun duct
7 Engine DB 603A-2 1750hp
8 Cannon Mk 103 30mm
9 Cannon cowling
10 2 cannons MG 151/A 20mm
11 Instrument panel
12 Windscreen
13 Control column
14 Right console
15 Canopy (open)
16 Right wing
17 Position light
18 Wing tank
19 Aileron
20 Aileron tab
21 Ejectable seat
22 Flap
23 Seat guides
24 Compressed air bottle
25 Fuel cap
26 Main tank 1850 litres
27 Air intake
28 Radio locator loop
29 Engine mountings
30 Engine DB 603A/2 1750hp
31 Extended propeller shaft
32 Stabilizer
33 Elevator
34 Fin structure
35 Fin

36 Rudder
37 Rudder structure
38 Trim tab
39 Rear spinner
40 Propeller (could be jettisoned in emergency)
41 Variable pitch mechanism
42 Elevator hinges
43 Spar
44 Elevator
45 Trim tab
46 Balance horn
47 Stabilizer
48 Structure
49 Ventral fin

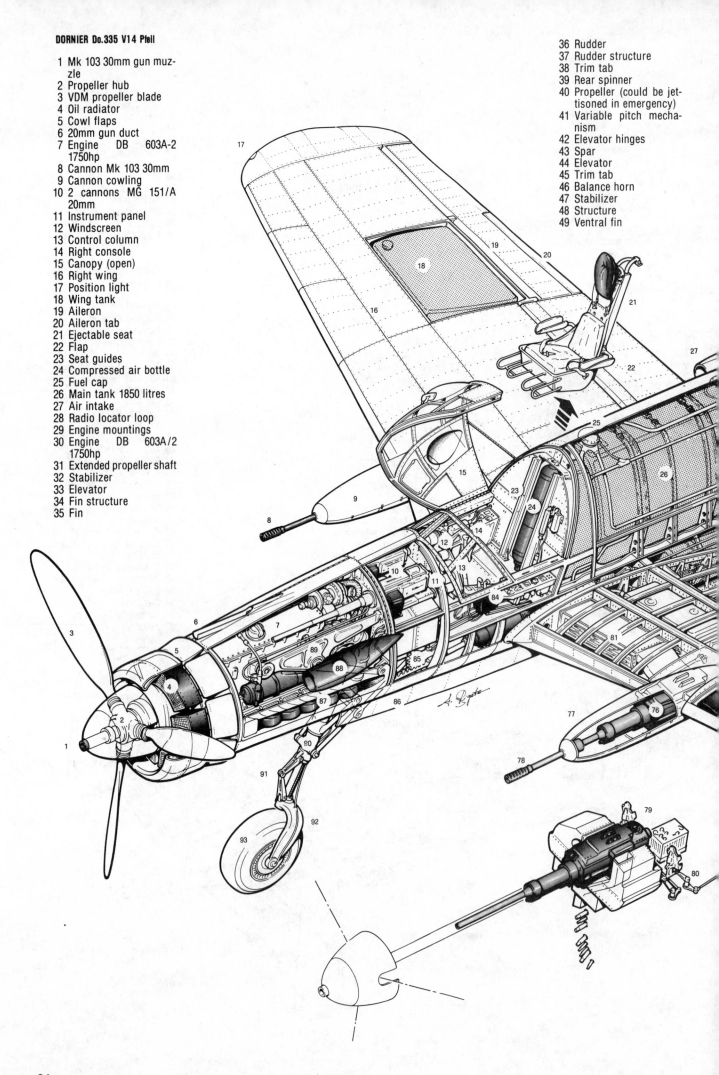

24

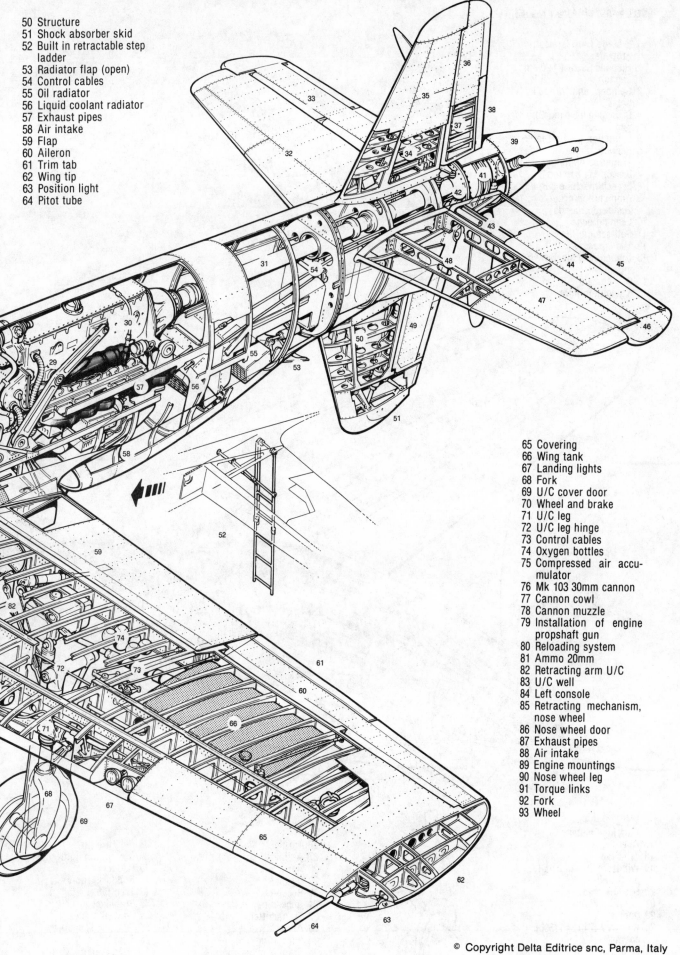

50 Structure
51 Shock absorber skid
52 Built in retractable step ladder
53 Radiator flap (open)
54 Control cables
55 Oil radiator
56 Liquid coolant radiator
57 Exhaust pipes
58 Air intake
59 Flap
60 Aileron
61 Trim tab
62 Wing tip
63 Position light
64 Pitot tube

65 Covering
66 Wing tank
67 Landing lights
68 Fork
69 U/C cover door
70 Wheel and brake
71 U/C leg
72 U/C leg hinge
73 Control cables
74 Oxygen bottles
75 Compressed air accumulator
76 Mk 103 30mm cannon
77 Cannon cowl
78 Cannon muzzle
79 Installation of engine propshaft gun
80 Reloading system
81 Ammo 20mm
82 Retracting arm U/C
83 U/C well
84 Left console
85 Retracting mechanism, nose wheel
86 Nose wheel door
87 Exhaust pipes
88 Air intake
89 Engine mountings
90 Nose wheel leg
91 Torque links
92 Fork
93 Wheel

BELL MODEL 14A P39D-1 Airacobra

1 3 blade Curtiss electric propeller
2 Hispano Suiza M1 20mm cannon
3 Spinner and propeller hub
4 Browning 0.5in machine gun muzzle
5 Reduction gear oil tank
6 Reduction gear (inside armoured container)
7 Breech M1 cannon
8 Breech machine gun (2)
9 Ammunition drum, 20mm (30 rounds)
10 Leading edge
11 Self-sealing tank
12 Mainspar
13 2 machine guns, Browning .303in
14 Gun barrels
15 Navigation light

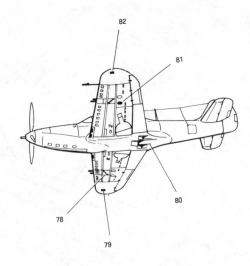

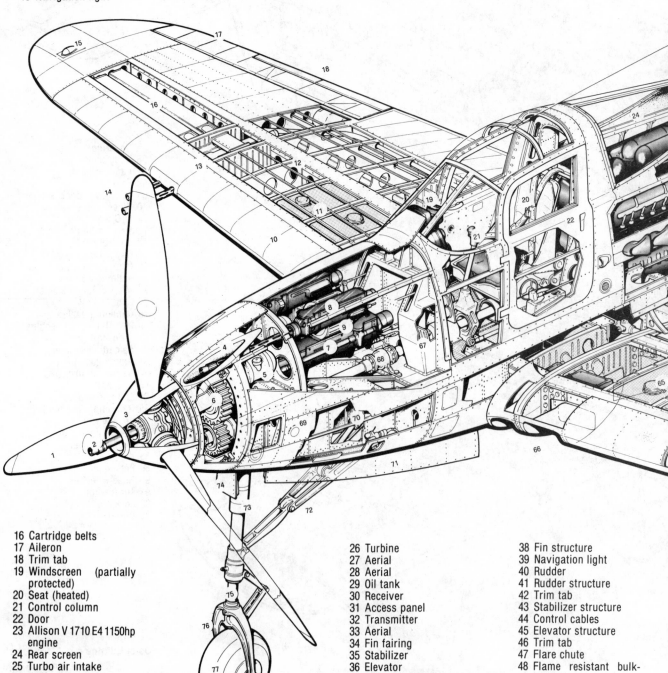

16 Cartridge belts
17 Aileron
18 Trim tab
19 Windscreen (partially protected)
20 Seat (heated)
21 Control column
22 Door
23 Allison V 1710 E4 1150hp engine
24 Rear screen
25 Turbo air intake

26 Turbine
27 Aerial
28 Aerial
29 Oil tank
30 Receiver
31 Access panel
32 Transmitter
33 Aerial
34 Fin fairing
35 Stabilizer
36 Elevator
37 Fin leading edge

38 Fin structure
39 Navigation light
40 Rudder
41 Rudder structure
42 Trim tab
43 Stabilizer structure
44 Control cables
45 Elevator structure
46 Trim tab
47 Flare chute
48 Flame resistant bulkhead

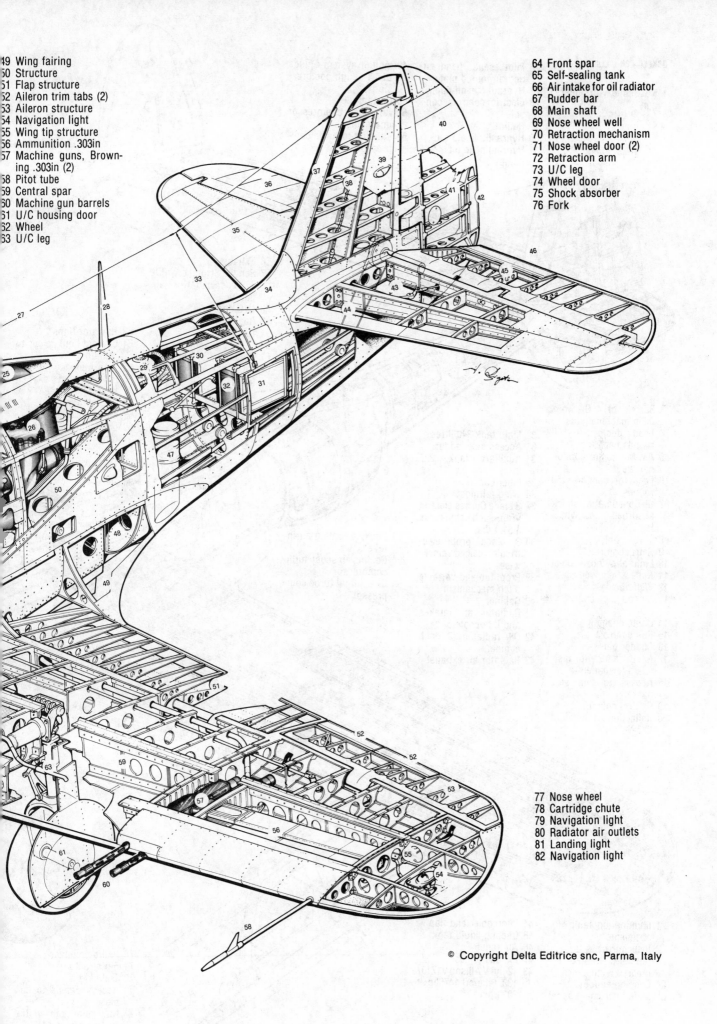

49 Wing fairing
50 Structure
51 Flap structure
52 Aileron trim tabs (2)
53 Aileron structure
54 Navigation light
55 Wing tip structure
56 Ammunition .303in
57 Machine guns, Browning .303in (2)
58 Pitot tube
59 Central spar
60 Machine gun barrels
61 U/C housing door
62 Wheel
63 U/C leg

64 Front spar
65 Self-sealing tank
66 Air intake for oil radiator
67 Rudder bar
68 Main shaft
69 Nose wheel well
70 Retraction mechanism
71 Nose wheel door (2)
72 Retraction arm
73 U/C leg
74 Wheel door
75 Shock absorber
76 Fork

77 Nose wheel
78 Cartridge chute
79 Navigation light
80 Radiator air outlets
81 Landing light
82 Navigation light

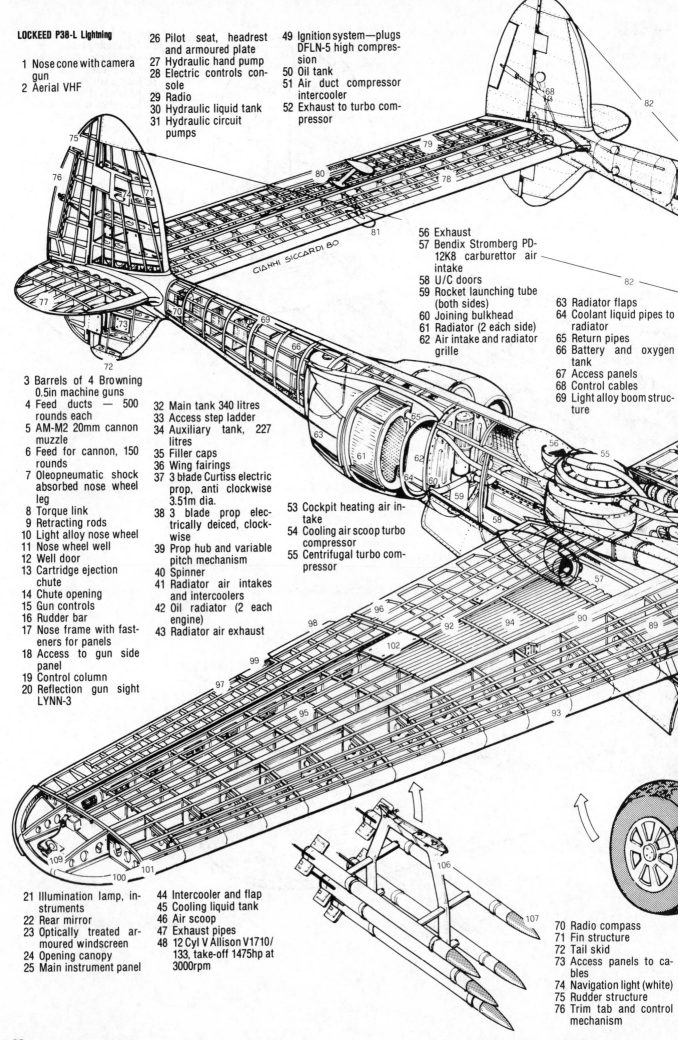

LOCKEED P38-L Lightning

1 Nose cone with camera gun
2 Aerial VHF

3 Barrels of 4 Browning 0.5in machine guns
4 Feed ducts — 500 rounds each
5 AM-M2 20mm cannon muzzle
6 Feed for cannon, 150 rounds
7 Oleopneumatic shock absorbed nose wheel leg
8 Torque link
9 Retracting rods
10 Light alloy nose wheel
11 Nose wheel well
12 Well door
13 Cartridge ejection chute
14 Chute opening
15 Gun controls
16 Rudder bar
17 Nose frame with fasteners for panels
18 Access to gun side panel
19 Control column
20 Reflection gun sight LYNN-3

21 Illumination lamp, instruments
22 Rear mirror
23 Optically treated armoured windscreen
24 Opening canopy
25 Main instrument panel

26 Pilot seat, headrest and armoured plate
27 Hydraulic hand pump
28 Electric controls console
29 Radio
30 Hydraulic liquid tank
31 Hydraulic circuit pumps

32 Main tank 340 litres
33 Access step ladder
34 Auxiliary tank, 227 litres
35 Filler caps
36 Wing fairings
37 3 blade Curtiss electric prop, anti clockwise 3.51m dia.
38 3 blade prop electrically deiced, clockwise
39 Prop hub and variable pitch mechanism
40 Spinner
41 Radiator air intakes and intercoolers
42 Oil radiator (2 each engine)
43 Radiator air exhaust

44 Intercooler and flap
45 Cooling liquid tank
46 Air scoop
47 Exhaust pipes
48 12 Cyl V Allison V1710/133, take-off 1475hp at 3000rpm

49 Ignition system—plugs DFLN-5 high compression
50 Oil tank
51 Air duct compressor intercooler
52 Exhaust to turbo compressor

53 Cockpit heating air intake
54 Cooling air scoop turbo compressor
55 Centrifugal turbo compressor

56 Exhaust
57 Bendix Stromberg PD-12K8 carburettor air intake
58 U/C doors
59 Rocket launching tube (both sides)
60 Joining bulkhead
61 Radiator (2 each side)
62 Air intake and radiator grille

63 Radiator flaps
64 Coolant liquid pipes to radiator
65 Return pipes
66 Battery and oxygen tank
67 Access panels
68 Control cables
69 Light alloy boom structure

70 Radio compass
71 Fin structure
72 Tail skid
73 Access panels to cables
74 Navigation light (white)
75 Rudder structure
76 Trim tab and control mechanism

GIANNI SICCARDI 80

28

77 Fixed stabilizer extension
78 Light alloy stabilizer,
metal skin
79 Elevator
80 Trim tab
81 Static balance top and
bottom
82 Aerials
83 Front bulkhead
84 Armoured flame resis-
tant bulkhead

95 Wing structure—ribs
tranversely stringered
96 Lockheed Fowler flap
—light alloy, in two
sections
97 Aileron—full length
hinge
98 Fixed trim tab
99 Trim tab
100 Wing tip (removable)
101 Joint
102 Access panels to cable
controls

103 Main U/C leg, hydrau-
lic shock absorber, re-
tracting rearwards
104 Torque link
105 Main wheel (smooth
surface)
106 Rocket pylon for 5
rockets
107 HVAR 5in. rocket
108 Pitot tube
109 Navigation light

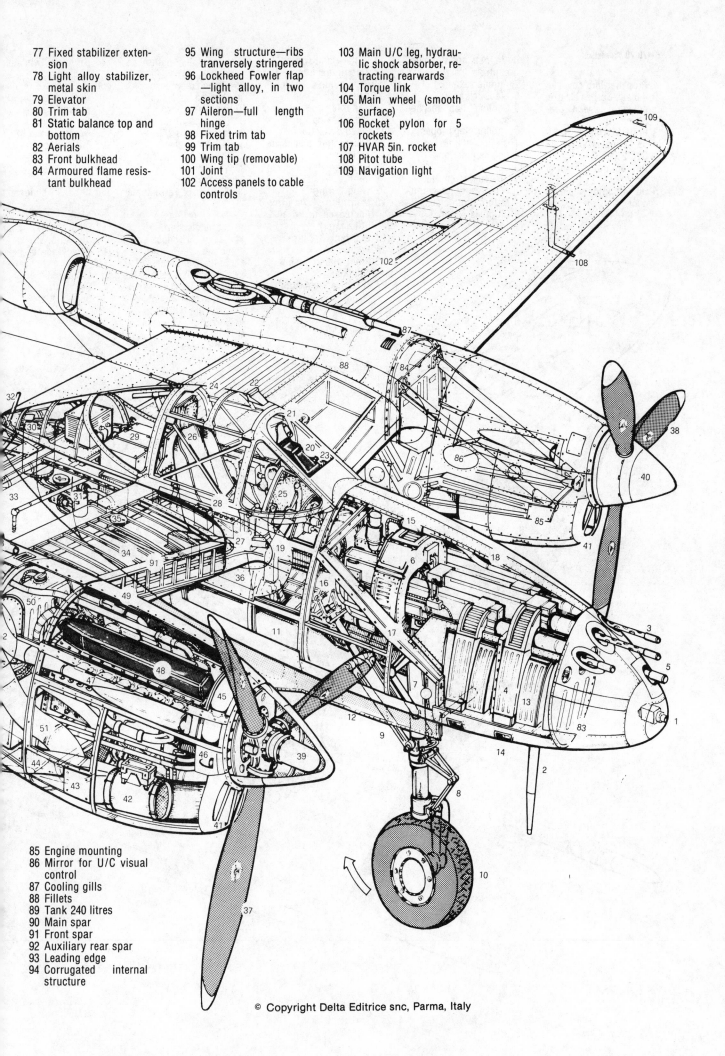

85 Engine mounting
86 Mirror for U/C visual
control
87 Cooling gills
88 Fillets
89 Tank 240 litres
90 Main spar
91 Front spar
92 Auxiliary rear spar
93 Leading edge
94 Corrugated internal
structure

P-47D-20 Thunderbolt

1 Propeller hub cover
2 4 blade Curtiss electric constant speed propeller
3 Pratt & Whitney R288-59 "Double Wasp" 18 Cyl. 2300hp
4 Oil radiator (on both sides)
5 Oil radiator cooling duct
6 Magnets and propeller controls
7 Annular exhaust
8 Flaps (closed)
9 Cooling flap mechanism
10 Cooling flaps (open)
11 Oil tank 108 litres
12 Engine mounting
13 Cowling
14 Air duct from turbo-compressor to carburettors (both sides)
15 Oil pipes
16 Battery and servos
17 Electric generator, de-icing pump & fuel level gauge
18 Variable opening oil radiator flap
19 Fixed deflector
20 Excess gas discharge outlet
21 Fuselage frame/wing joint
22 Wing fairing
23 Main tank 776 litres (increased up to 1022 litres later)
24 U/C tank 378 litres
25 Radio
26 Front flame resistant bulkhead
27 Turbo exhaust hood
28 Intercooler outlet on both sides
29 Turbo compressor
30 Cooling air ducts
31 Oxygen bottles
32 Compressor air filter
33 Intercoolers
34 Rudder cables
35 Elevator cables
36 VHF aerial
37 Fin fairing
38 Tail wheel, retractable and steerable
39 Tail wheel doors
40 Static discharge rod
41 Tailwheel shock absorber
42 Tail wheel pivot
43 Retracting mechanism
44 Elevator control bar
45 Stabilizer—metal structure with 2 spars
46 Elevator metal skin
47 Trim tab
48 Tab cables
49 Structure twin spar and ribs
50 Rudder — 1 deg right—to compens torque
51 Rudder tab
52 Navigation light
53 Turbo duct
54 Lifting point
55 Tail wheel supp frame
56 Canopy, slides ba wards
57 Rails
58 Pilot seat, headr and safety belts
59 Armoured bulkhead
60 Front windscree armoured glass
61 Rear mirror
62 Dashboard

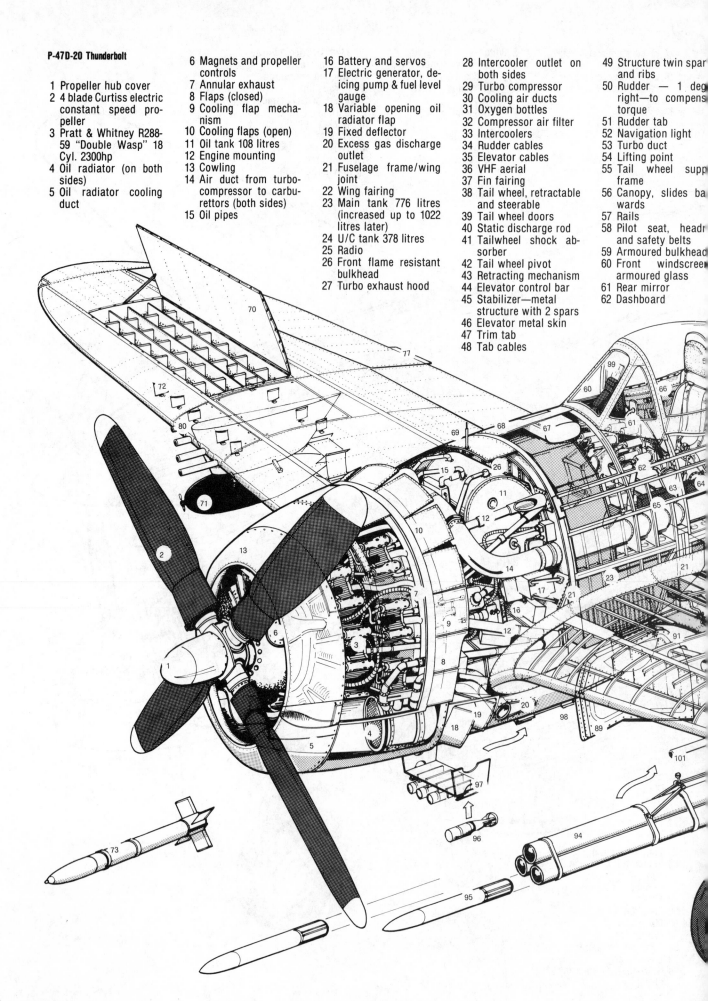

30

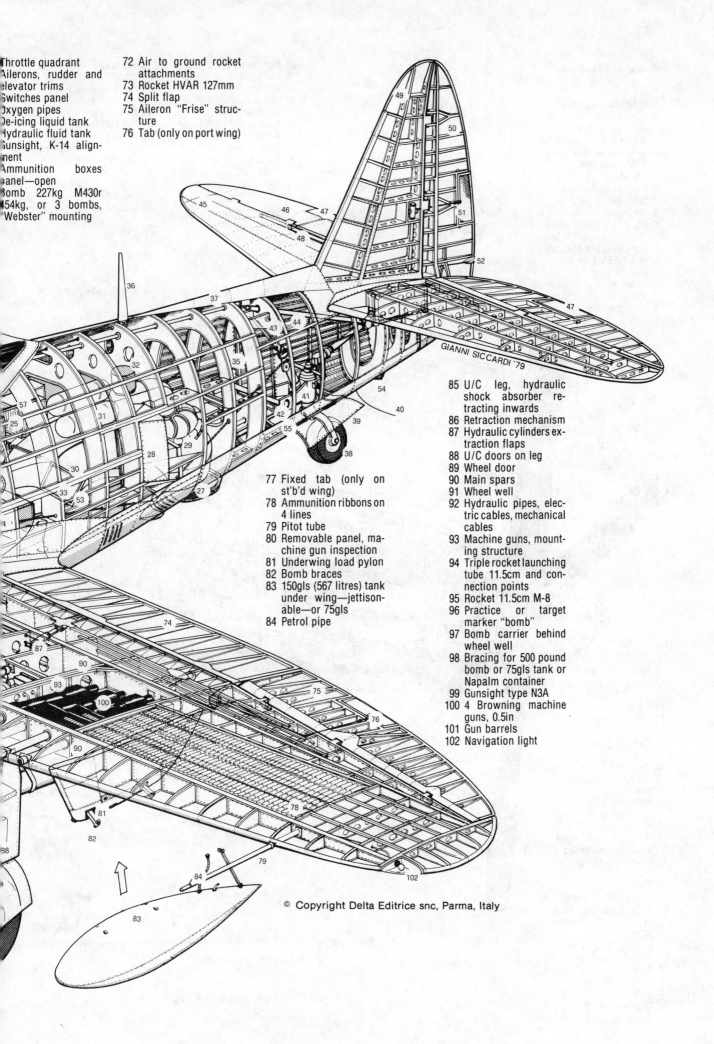

Throttle quadrant
Ailerons, rudder and elevator trims
Switches panel
Oxygen pipes
De-icing liquid tank
Hydraulic fluid tank
Gunsight, K-14 alignment
Ammunition boxes panel—open
Bomb 227kg M430r 454kg, or 3 bombs, "Webster" mounting

72 Air to ground rocket attachments
73 Rocket HVAR 127mm
74 Split flap
75 Aileron "Frise" structure
76 Tab (only on port wing)

77 Fixed tab (only on st'b'd wing)
78 Ammunition ribbons on 4 lines
79 Pitot tube
80 Removable panel, machine gun inspection
81 Underwing load pylon
82 Bomb braces
83 150gls (567 litres) tank under wing—jettisonable—or 75gls
84 Petrol pipe

85 U/C leg, hydraulic shock absorber retracting inwards
86 Retraction mechanism
87 Hydraulic cylinders extraction flaps
88 U/C doors on leg
89 Wheel door
90 Main spars
91 Wheel well
92 Hydraulic pipes, electric cables, mechanical cables
93 Machine guns, mounting structure
94 Triple rocket launching tube 11.5cm and connection points
95 Rocket 11.5cm M-8
96 Practice or target marker "bomb"
97 Bomb carrier behind wheel well
98 Bracing for 500 pound bomb or 75gls tank or Napalm container
99 Gunsight type N3A
100 4 Browning machine guns, 0.5in
101 Gun barrels
102 Navigation light

GIANNI SICCARDI '79

North American P-51D Mustang

1 Propeller hub cover
2 Hamilton standard hydromatic propeller 3.40m dia. constant speed, variable pitch. 1.45 degrees downthrust
3 Cooling liquid tank
4 Carburettor air duct
5 Air intake
6 Packard V-1650-7 liquid cooled engine 12 Cyl Vee 1450hp on take off and 1695hp max in emergency
7 Panel around exhaust pipes
8 Engine mounting

9 Rear radiator and turbo compressor, 2 stage, 2 speeds
10 Oil tank
11 Front armoured bulkhead
12 Canopy sliding backward
13 Instrument panel
14 Canopy opening control
15 Instrument light
16 Adjustable pilot seat and harness
17 Headrest and rear armoured bulkhead
18 Electrical circuit indicator panel
19 Battery
20 Radio compartment
21 Trim controls, rudder, ailerons and carburettor
22 Landing gear lever
23 Throttle quadrant
24 Rudder bar
25 Control column
26 Armoured bulkhead
27 Engine cowling

28 Hydraulic liquid tank
29 Flat armoured windscreen
30 Gunsight, Bell & Howe 11 N9 or K14
31 Aerial connected to armoured plate, through canopy
32 Fuselage auxiliary tank, 322 litres and filler cap

33 Electrical socket (for ground connection)
34 Oxygen bottles
35 Air intake
36 Oil radiator
37 Coolant radiator
38 Adjustable air outlet
39 Oil and coolant pipes
40 Control cables
41 Canopy rails
42 Fuselage strengthening frames
43 Dual aerial masts
44 Main fuselage longerons
45 Lifting point
46 Tail wheel—retracts forward
47 Tail wheel doors
48 Shock absorber and steering and retracting mechanism

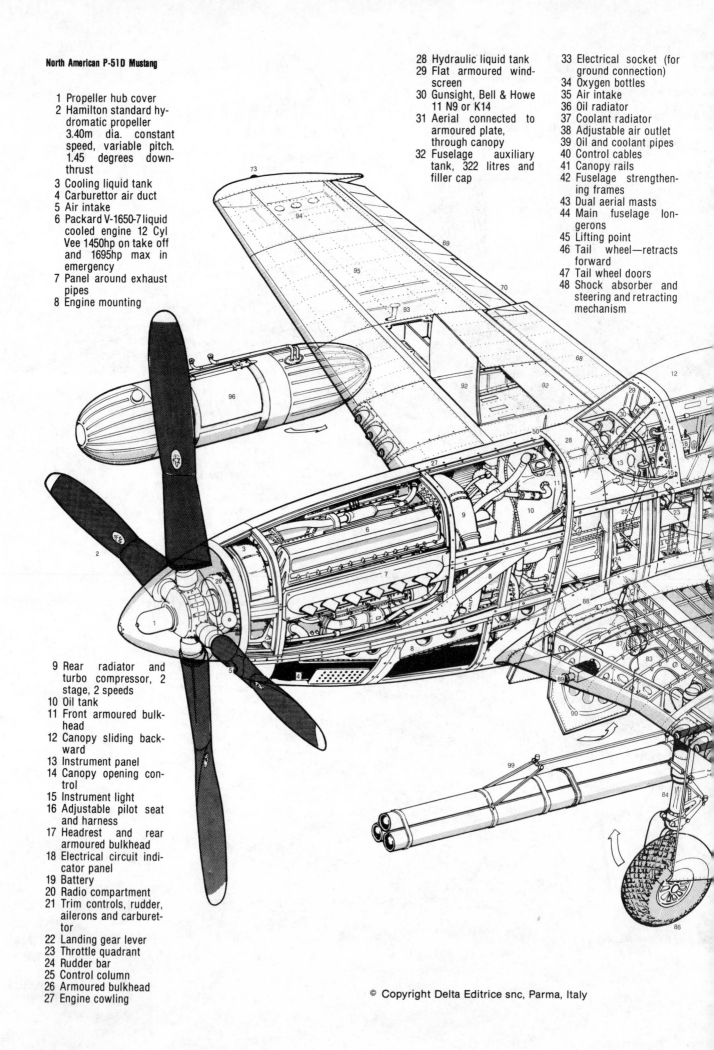

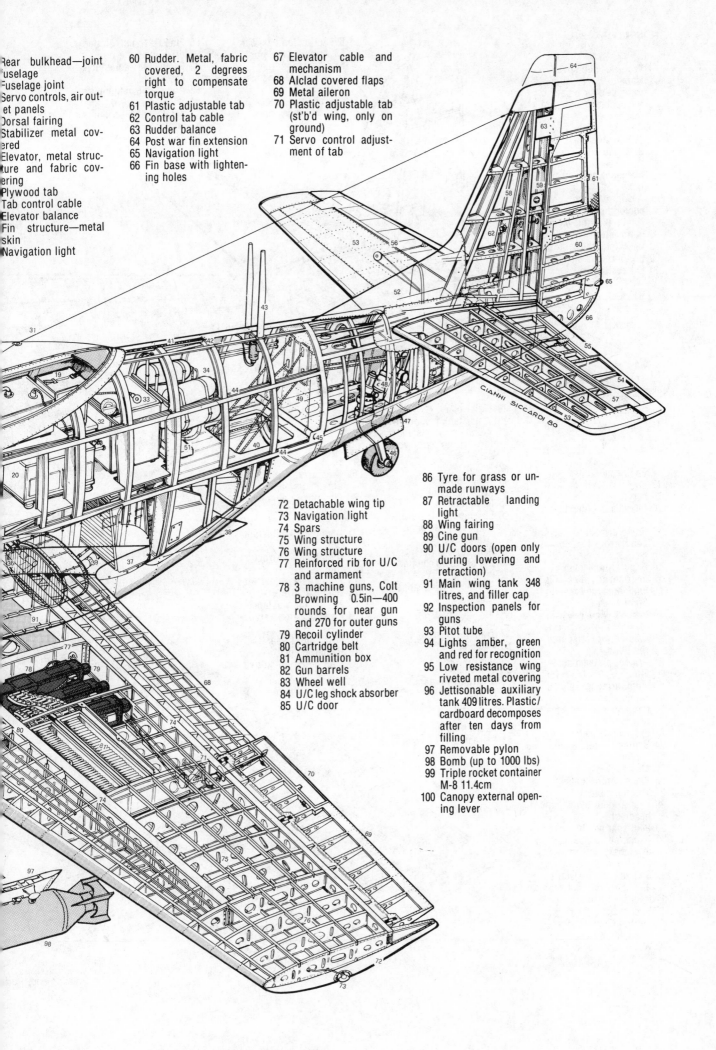

Rear bulkhead—joint fuselage
Fuselage joint
Servo controls, air outlet panels
Dorsal fairing
Stabilizer metal covered
Elevator, metal structure and fabric covering
Plywood tab
Tab control cable
Elevator balance
Fin structure—metal skin
Navigation light

60 Rudder. Metal, fabric covered, 2 degrees right to compensate torque
61 Plastic adjustable tab
62 Control tab cable
63 Rudder balance
64 Post war fin extension
65 Navigation light
66 Fin base with lightening holes

67 Elevator cable and mechanism
68 Alclad covered flaps
69 Metal aileron
70 Plastic adjustable tab (st'b'd wing, only on ground)
71 Servo control adjustment of tab

72 Detachable wing tip
73 Navigation light
74 Spars
75 Wing structure
76 Wing structure
77 Reinforced rib for U/C and armament
78 3 machine guns, Colt Browning 0.5in—400 rounds for near gun and 270 for outer guns
79 Recoil cylinder
80 Cartridge belt
81 Ammunition box
82 Gun barrels
83 Wheel well
84 U/C leg shock absorber
85 U/C door

86 Tyre for grass or unmade runways
87 Retractable landing light
88 Wing fairing
89 Cine gun
90 U/C doors (open only during lowering and retraction)
91 Main wing tank 348 litres, and filler cap
92 Inspection panels for guns
93 Pitot tube
94 Lights amber, green and red for recognition
95 Low resistance wing riveted metal covering
96 Jettisonable auxiliary tank 409 litres. Plastic/cardboard decomposes after ten days from filling
97 Removable pylon
98 Bomb (up to 1000 lbs)
99 Triple rocket container M-8 11.4cm
100 Canopy external opening lever

1 Propeller hub cover
2 Hamilton 3 blade variable pitch propeller
3 Reduction gears and magnetos
4 Cowling
5 18 cyl. air cooled Pratt & Whitney 2200hp radial engine water-methanol injection system
6 Air intake and intercooler duct
7 Air intake and oil radiator duct
8 Open flaps and controls
9 Bottom flaps closed
10 Exhaust pipes

11 Armour plate protected oil tank
12 Oil tank 72 litres
13 Coolant tank
14 Engine mounting
15 Engine controls and servos
16 Oil radiator, intercooler air escape and flap
17 Front armoured bulkhead, protecting cockpit
18 Front armour plate
19 Instrument panel—illuminated red for night flight
20 Curved windscreen in Plexiglas—later substituted with armoured flat plate
21 Armour plated glass—later substituted with single armoured plated windscreen
22 Canopy sliding rearwards
23 Exhaust deflector
24 Bottom oil radiator protection
25 Map pocket
26 Radio control panel
27 Throttle quadrant
28 Rear armour plate and headrest
29 Pilot seat and harness
30 Morse apparatus
31 Incendiary device
32 Fire extinguisher
33 Console for electric and hydraulic controls
34 Hydraulic hand pump
35 Rudder bar
36 Control column
37 Rear side window
38 Water tank for engine ignition

39 Water pipe
40 Water tank mounting
41 Aerial mast (leaning forward on early version)
42 Aerial
43 Whip aerial
44 Identification light
45 Navigation light
46 Fuselage structure—frames and aluminium stringers
47 Radio compartment
48 Bottom radio compartment
49 Self destroying apparatus
50 Handle and step
51 Batteries
52 Transverse stringers
53 Radio compass
54 Control cables
55 Transmitter
56 Ventral whip aerial
57 Oxygen bottle
58 Filler cap
59 Gun sight
60 Rear lifting point
61 Retractable rear wheel, solid rubber

62 Retraction cylinder
63 Armour steel door
64 Shock absorber
65 Wheel steering mechanism
66 Tail wheel mounting
67 Arrestor hook (retracted)

68 Arrestor hook (extended position)
69 Stabilizer structure, aluminium alloy
70 Elevator, aluminium structure, fabric covered
71 Aluminium adjustable tab
72 Aluminium structure rudder
73 Adjustable rudder tab
74 Diagonal stringers
75 Rudder horn balance
76 Fin structure metal covered
77 Fin support spar
78 Rudder hinges
79 Flap (internal) slotted

80 Flap (external) slotted
81 Frise type aileron
82 Fixed tab adjustable on ground
83 Adjustable in flight tab
84 Wing structure, aluminium ribs, stringers and spar

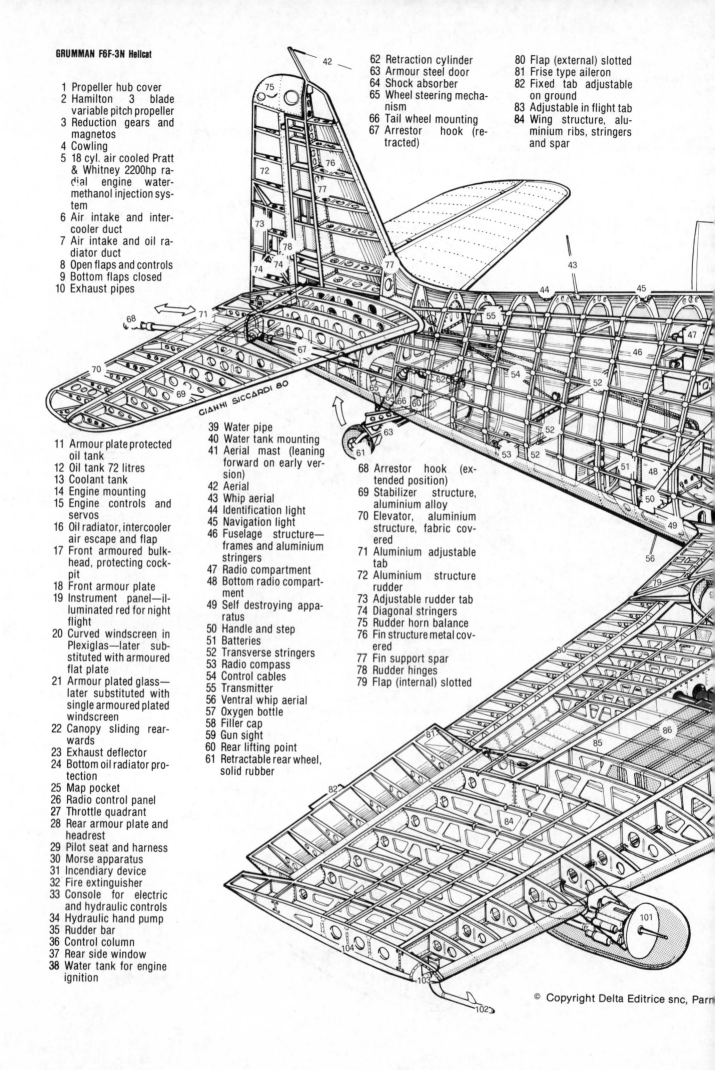

GIAHHI SICCARDI 80

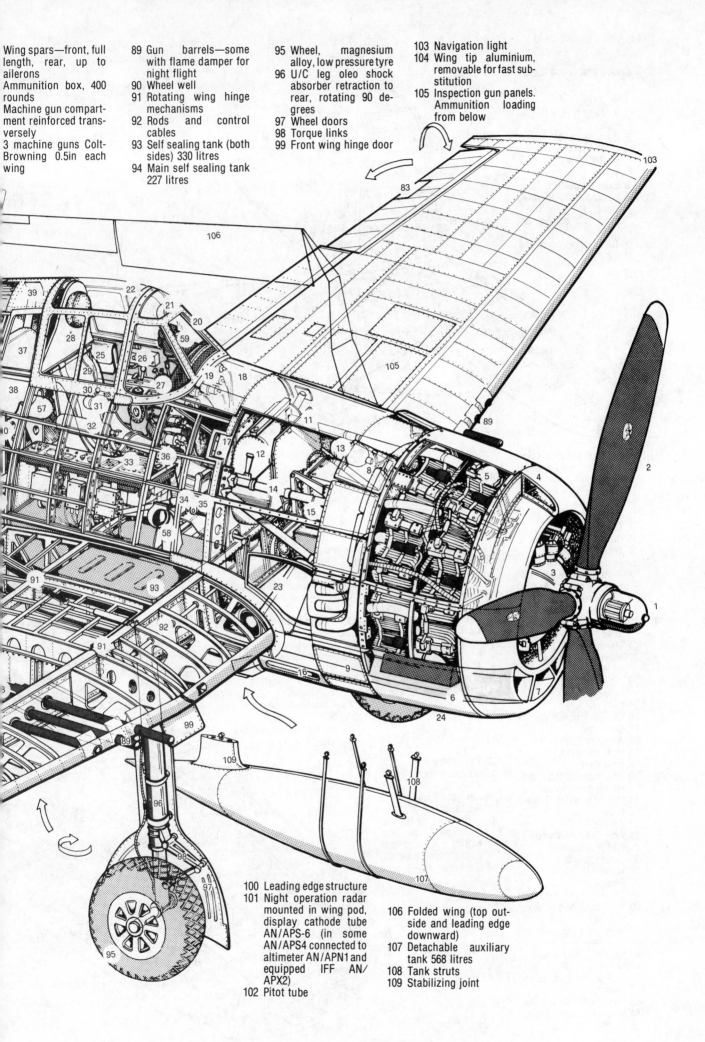

Wing spars—front, full length, rear, up to ailerons

Ammunition box, 400 rounds

Machine gun compartment reinforced transversely

3 machine guns Colt-Browning 0.5in each wing

89 Gun barrels—some with flame damper for night flight
90 Wheel well
91 Rotating wing hinge mechanisms
92 Rods and control cables
93 Self sealing tank (both sides) 330 litres
94 Main self sealing tank 227 litres

95 Wheel, magnesium alloy, low pressure tyre
96 U/C leg oleo shock absorber retraction to rear, rotating 90 degrees
97 Wheel doors
98 Torque links
99 Front wing hinge door

103 Navigation light
104 Wing tip aluminium, removable for fast substitution
105 Inspection gun panels. Ammunition loading from below

100 Leading edge structure
101 Night operation radar mounted in wing pod, display cathode tube AN/APS-6 (in some AN/APS4 connected to altimeter AN/APN1 and equipped IFF AN/APX2)
102 Pitot tube

106 Folded wing (top outside and leading edge downward)
107 Detachable auxiliary tank 568 litres
108 Tank struts
109 Stabilizing joint

1 Propeller hub
2 4 blade Hamilton propeller
3 Carburettor air intake
4 Pratt & Whitney engine R-2800-18W "C" Twin Wasp 18 Cylinders
5 Exhaust pipes
6 Hydraulically operated cowl flaps
7 Side and bottom exhausts
8 Turbo compressor and air duct

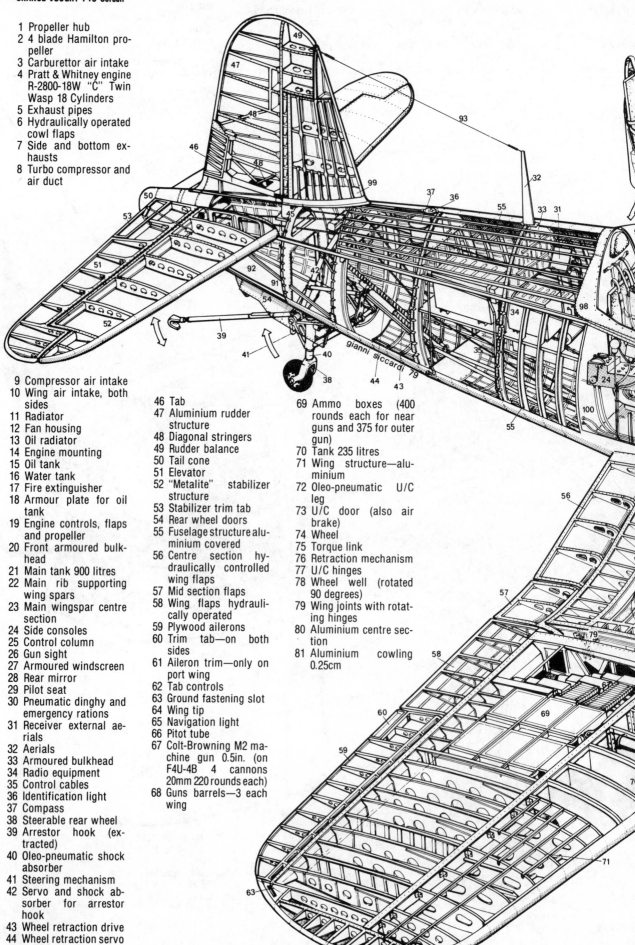

gianni siccardi 79

9 Compressor air intake
10 Wing air intake, both sides
11 Radiator
12 Fan housing
13 Oil radiator
14 Engine mounting
15 Oil tank
16 Water tank
17 Fire extinguisher
18 Armour plate for oil tank
19 Engine controls, flaps and propeller
20 Front armoured bulkhead
21 Main tank 900 litres
22 Main rib supporting wing spars
23 Main wingspar centre section
24 Side consoles
25 Control column
26 Gun sight
27 Armoured windscreen
28 Rear mirror
29 Pilot seat
30 Pneumatic dinghy and emergency rations
31 Receiver external aerials
32 Aerials
33 Armoured bulkhead
34 Radio equipment
35 Control cables
36 Identification light
37 Compass
38 Steerable rear wheel
39 Arrestor hook (extracted)
40 Oleo-pneumatic shock absorber
41 Steering mechanism
42 Servo and shock absorber for arrestor hook
43 Wheel retraction drive
44 Wheel retraction servo
45 Rudder hinge

46 Tab
47 Aluminium rudder structure
48 Diagonal stringers
49 Rudder balance
50 Tail cone
51 Elevator
52 "Metalite" stabilizer structure
53 Stabilizer trim tab
54 Rear wheel doors
55 Fuselage structure aluminium covered
56 Centre section hydraulically controlled wing flaps
57 Mid section flaps
58 Wing flaps hydraulically operated
59 Plywood ailerons
60 Trim tab—on both sides
61 Aileron trim—only on port wing
62 Tab controls
63 Ground fastening slot
64 Wing tip
65 Navigation light
66 Pitot tube
67 Colt-Browning M2 machine gun 0.5in. (on F4U-4B 4 cannons 20mm 220 rounds each)
68 Guns barrels—3 each wing

69 Ammo boxes (400 rounds each for near guns and 375 for outer gun)
70 Tank 235 litres
71 Wing structure—aluminium
72 Oleo-pneumatic U/C leg
73 U/C door (also air brake)
74 Wheel
75 Torque link
76 Retraction mechanism
77 U/C hinges
78 Wheel well (rotated 90 degrees)
79 Wing joints with rotating hinges
80 Aluminium centre section
81 Aluminium cowling 0.25cm

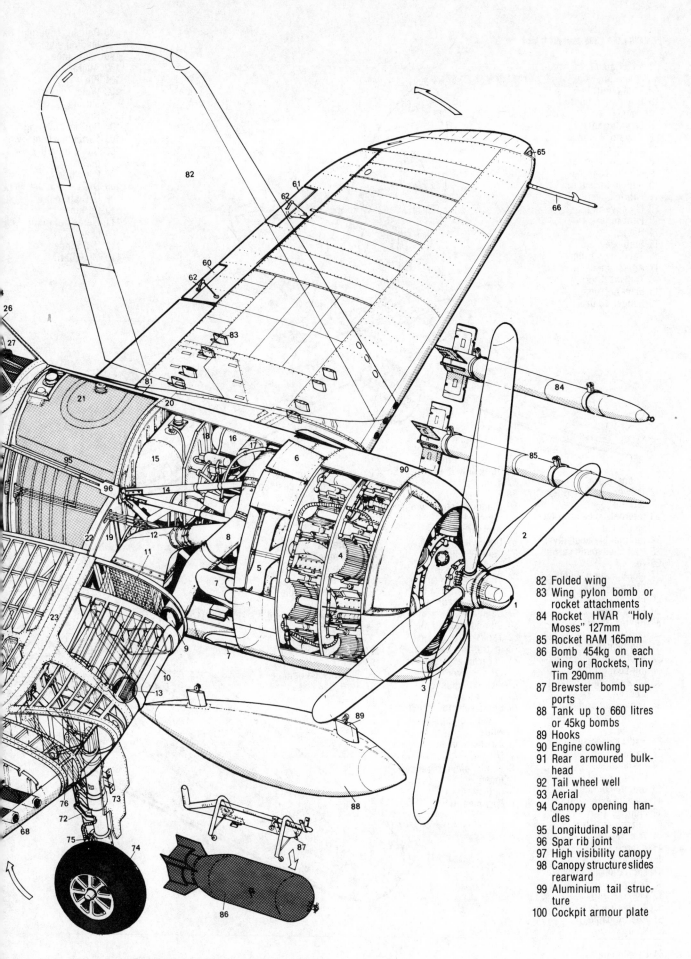

82 Folded wing
83 Wing pylon bomb or rocket attachments
84 Rocket HVAR "Holy Moses" 127mm
85 Rocket RAM 165mm
86 Bomb 454kg on each wing or Rockets, Tiny Tim 290mm
87 Brewster bomb supports
88 Tank up to 660 litres or 45kg bombs
89 Hooks
90 Engine cowling
91 Rear armoured bulkhead
92 Tail wheel well
93 Aerial
94 Canopy opening handles
95 Longitudinal spar
96 Spar rib joint
97 High visibility canopy
98 Canopy structure slides rearward
99 Aluminium tail structure
100 Cockpit armour plate

DE HAVILLAND DH98 Mosquito B Mk IV

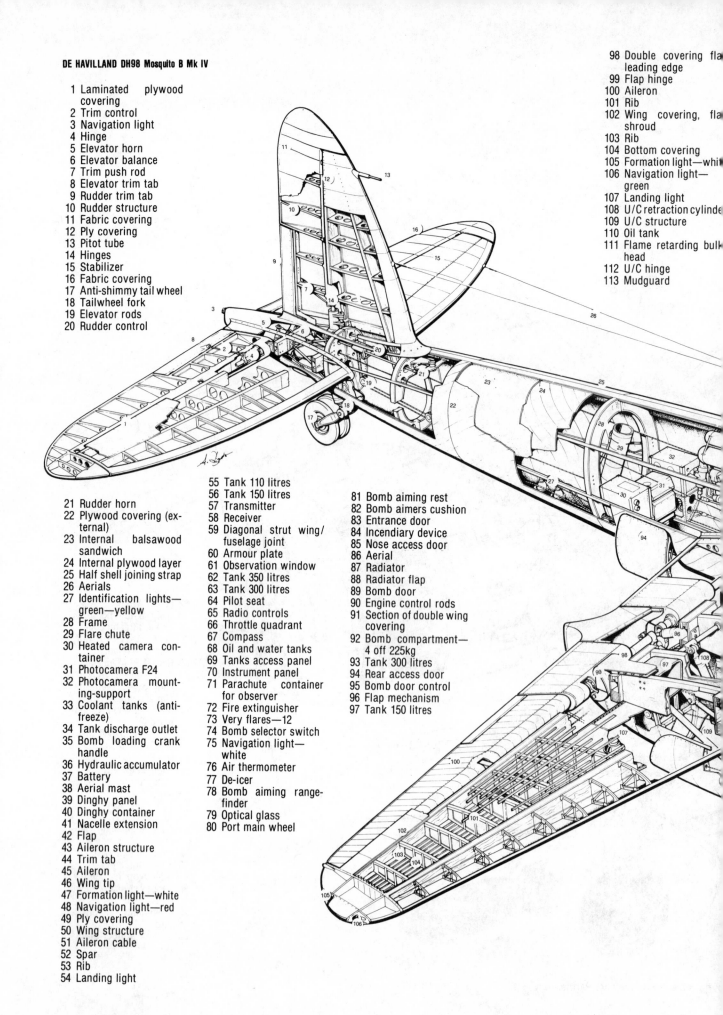

1 Laminated plywood covering
2 Trim control
3 Navigation light
4 Hinge
5 Elevator horn
6 Elevator balance
7 Trim push rod
8 Elevator trim tab
9 Rudder trim tab
10 Rudder structure
11 Fabric covering
12 Ply covering
13 Pitot tube
14 Hinges
15 Stabilizer
16 Fabric covering
17 Anti-shimmy tail wheel
18 Tailwheel fork
19 Elevator rods
20 Rudder control

21 Rudder horn
22 Plywood covering (external)
23 Internal balsawood sandwich
24 Internal plywood layer
25 Half shell joining strap
26 Aerials
27 Identification lights— green—yellow
28 Frame
29 Flare chute
30 Heated camera container
31 Photocamera F24
32 Photocamera mounting-support
33 Coolant tanks (antifreeze)
34 Tank discharge outlet
35 Bomb loading crank handle
36 Hydraulic accumulator
37 Battery
38 Aerial mast
39 Dinghy panel
40 Dinghy container
41 Nacelle extension
42 Flap
43 Aileron structure
44 Trim tab
45 Aileron
46 Wing tip
47 Formation light—white
48 Navigation light—red
49 Ply covering
50 Wing structure
51 Aileron cable
52 Spar
53 Rib
54 Landing light

55 Tank 110 litres
56 Tank 150 litres
57 Transmitter
58 Receiver
59 Diagonal strut wing/ fuselage joint
60 Armour plate
61 Observation window
62 Tank 350 litres
63 Tank 300 litres
64 Pilot seat
65 Radio controls
66 Throttle quadrant
67 Compass
68 Oil and water tanks
69 Tanks access panel
70 Instrument panel
71 Parachute container for observer
72 Fire extinguisher
73 Very flares—12
74 Bomb selector switch
75 Navigation light— white
76 Air thermometer
77 De-icer
78 Bomb aiming rangefinder
79 Optical glass
80 Port main wheel

81 Bomb aiming rest
82 Bomb aimers cushion
83 Entrance door
84 Incendiary device
85 Nose access door
86 Aerial
87 Radiator
88 Radiator flap
89 Bomb door
90 Engine control rods
91 Section of double wing covering
92 Bomb compartment— 4 off 225kg
93 Tank 300 litres
94 Rear access door
95 Bomb door control
96 Flap mechanism
97 Tank 150 litres

98 Double covering fla leading edge
99 Flap hinge
100 Aileron
101 Rib
102 Wing covering, fla shroud
103 Rib
104 Bottom covering
105 Formation light—whi
106 Navigation light— green
107 Landing light
108 U/C retraction cylinde
109 U/C structure
110 Oil tank
111 Flame retarding bulk head
112 U/C hinge
113 Mudguard

114 Engine mounting—supercharger behind
115 Shock absorber—rubber blocks inside
116 Shock absorber gaiter
117 Wheel brake and tyre
118 Carburettor air intake
119 Fishtail exhaust stacks
120 Merlin XXI engine
121 Coolant header tank
122 Variable pitch mechanism
123 Propeller hub
124 Spinner
125 DeHavilland Hydromatic 3 blade propeller

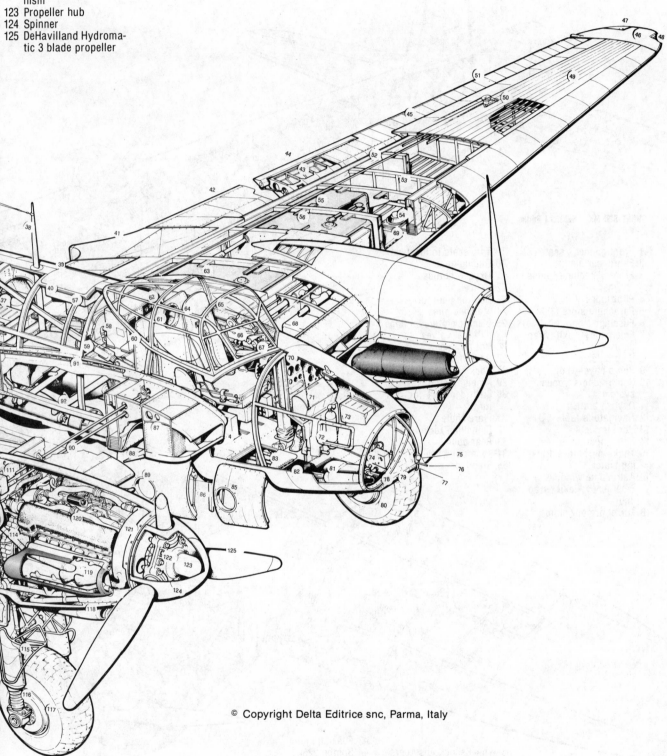

39

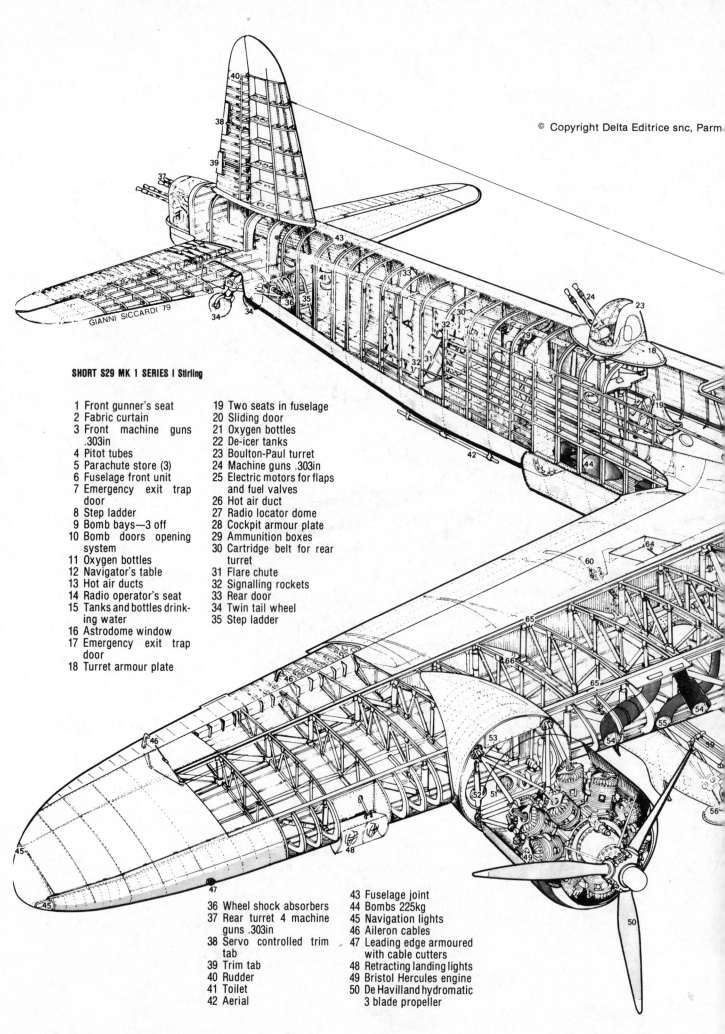

© Copyright Delta Editrice snc, Parm

GIANNI SICCARDI '79

SHORT S29 MK 1 SERIES I Stirling

1 Front gunner's seat
2 Fabric curtain
3 Front machine guns .303in
4 Pitot tubes
5 Parachute store (3)
6 Fuselage front unit
7 Emergency exit trap door
8 Step ladder
9 Bomb bays—3 off
10 Bomb doors opening system
11 Oxygen bottles
12 Navigator's table
13 Hot air ducts
14 Radio operator's seat
15 Tanks and bottles drinking water
16 Astrodome window
17 Emergency exit trap door
18 Turret armour plate

19 Two seats in fuselage
20 Sliding door
21 Oxygen bottles
22 De-icer tanks
23 Boulton-Paul turret
24 Machine guns .303in
25 Electric motors for flaps and fuel valves
26 Hot air duct
27 Radio locator dome
28 Cockpit armour plate
29 Ammunition boxes
30 Cartridge belt for rear turret
31 Flare chute
32 Signalling rockets
33 Rear door
34 Twin tail wheel
35 Step ladder

36 Wheel shock absorbers
37 Rear turret 4 machine guns .303in
38 Servo controlled trim tab
39 Trim tab
40 Rudder
41 Toilet
42 Aerial

43 Fuselage joint
44 Bombs 225kg
45 Navigation lights
46 Aileron cables
47 Leading edge armoured with cable cutters
48 Retracting landing lights
49 Bristol Hercules engine
50 De Havilland hydromatic 3 blade propeller

40

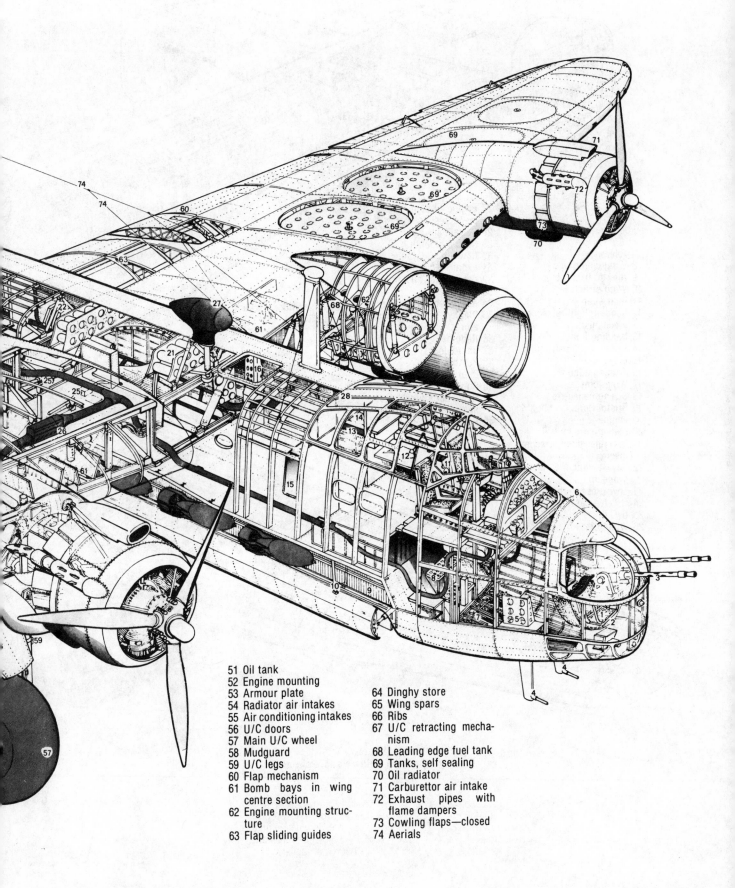

51 Oil tank
52 Engine mounting
53 Armour plate
54 Radiator air intakes
55 Air conditioning intakes
56 U/C doors
57 Main U/C wheel
58 Mudguard
59 U/C legs
60 Flap mechanism
61 Bomb bays in wing centre section
62 Engine mounting structure
63 Flap sliding guides

64 Dinghy store
65 Wing spars
66 Ribs
67 U/C retracting mechanism
68 Leading edge fuel tank
69 Tanks, self sealing
70 Oil radiator
71 Carburettor air intake
72 Exhaust pipes with flame dampers
73 Cowling flaps—closed
74 Aerials

HANDLEY PAGE Halifax B MK III

1 Wing tip
2 Navigation light—green
3 Navigation light—green
4 Wing tip structure
5 Wing structure
6 Aileron static balance

7 Aileron
8 Wing covering
9 Aileron trim tab
10 Wing structure
11 Rear spar
12 Landing light retraction mechanism
13 Landing lights
14 Leading edge structure
15 Front spar
16 Trailing edge
17 Wing joint
18 Strengthened rib
19 Bristol Hercules Mk XVI engine
20 Reduction gear
21 Variable pitch mechanism
22 De Havilland 3 blade propeller
23 Low pressure tyre
24 U/C leg casting
25 U/C door
26 Wing joint

27 Engine mount attachment to spar
28 Retraction ram
29 Engine mounting
30 Cowling
31 Exhaust manifold
32 Carburettor air intake
33 Rear spar
34 Rear wing unit structure
35 Dinghy and lifebelt stores
36 Radome
37 Bomb doors
38 Bomb (245kg)
39 Door retraction cylinder
40 Co-pilot's seat
41 Radio operator's seat and radio equipment
42 Folding seat and navigator's table
43 Aerial
44 Pitot tube

45 Nose gun Vickers K .303in
46 Ammunition channel to nose gun
47 Control column
48 Pilot seat
49 Astrodome
50 Batteries
51 Throttle quadrant

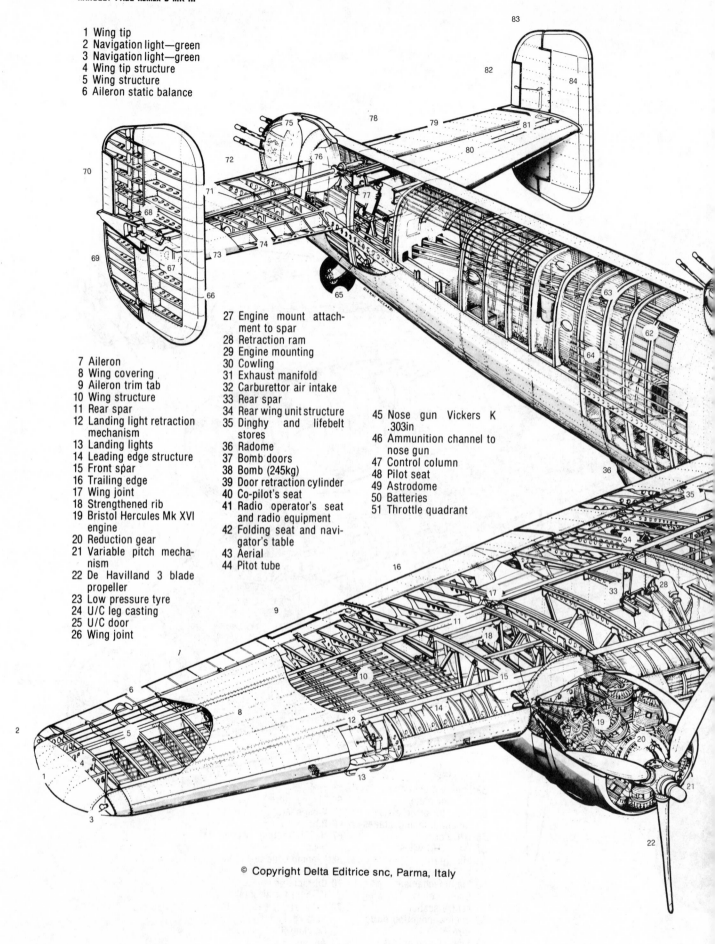

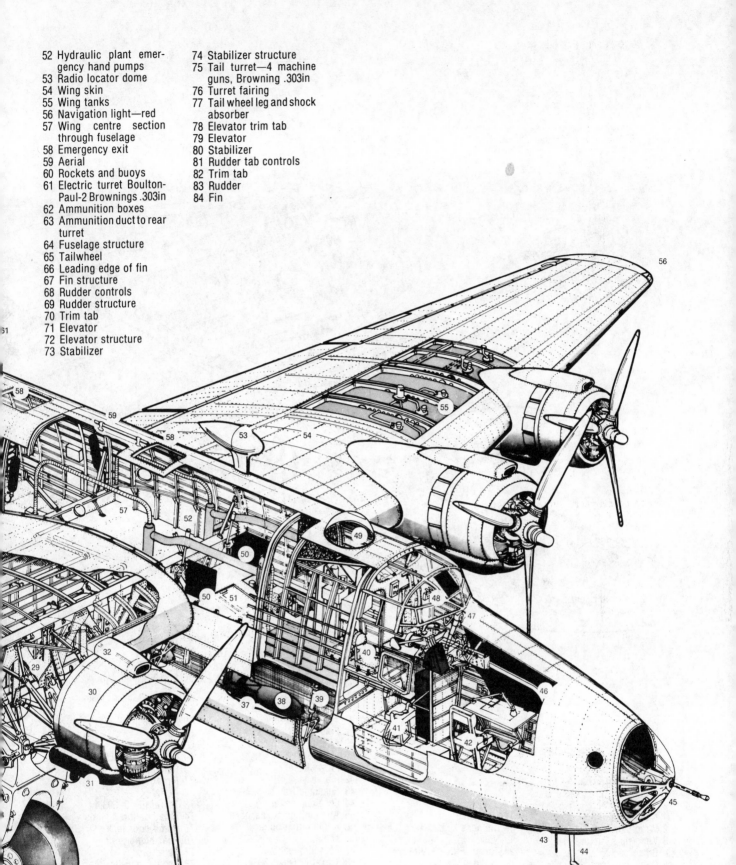

52 Hydraulic plant emer-
   gency hand pumps
53 Radio locator dome
54 Wing skin
55 Wing tanks
56 Navigation light—red
57 Wing centre section
   through fuselage
58 Emergency exit
59 Aerial
60 Rockets and buoys
61 Electric turret Boulton-
   Paul-2 Brownings .303in
62 Ammunition boxes
63 Ammunition duct to rear
   turret
64 Fuselage structure
65 Tailwheel
66 Leading edge of fin
67 Fin structure
68 Rudder controls
69 Rudder structure
70 Trim tab
71 Elevator
72 Elevator structure
73 Stabilizer

74 Stabilizer structure
75 Tail turret—4 machine
   guns, Browning .303in
76 Turret fairing
77 Tail wheel leg and shock
   absorber
78 Elevator trim tab
79 Elevator
80 Stabilizer
81 Rudder tab controls
82 Trim tab
83 Rudder
84 Fin

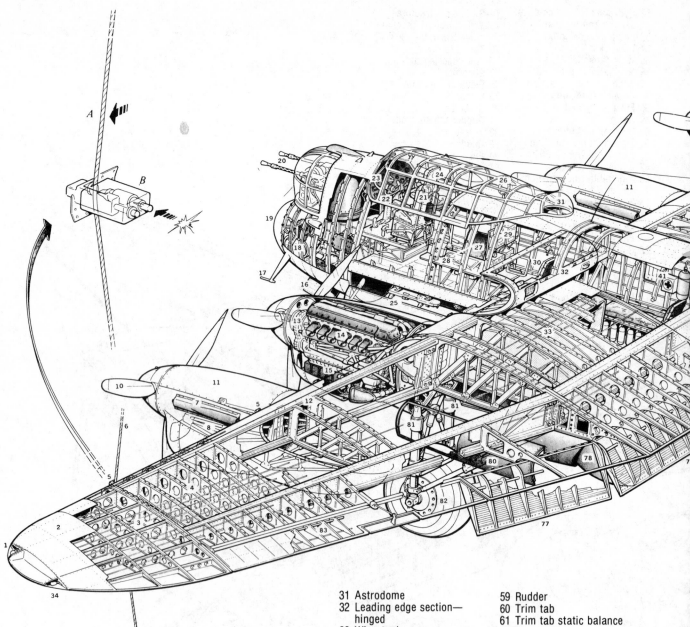

AVRO TYPE 638 Lancaster MK I

1 Navigation light
2 Wing skin
3 Wing tip structure
4 Ribs
5 Cable cutter device
6 Balloon cable
7 Flame damper
8 Engine RR Merlin 22
9 Spinner
10 3 blade metal propeller
11 Engine cowling
12 Front spar
13 Reduction gears
14 Exhaust pipes
15 Radiator
16 Door

17 Pitot tube
18 Gunner's seat
19 Nose
20 Turret FN5, 2 Vickers .303in
21 Pilot seat, armour plate, oxygen
22 Control column
23 Instrument panel
24 Armoured headrest
25 Bomb bay door
26 Radio locator loop
27 Navigator's seat
28 Navigator's table
29 Radio equipment
30 Radio operator's seat

31 Astrodome
32 Leading edge section— hinged
33 Wing tank
34 Formation light
35 Aileron
36 Trim tab adjustable
37 Tab control rod
38 Fixed tab
39 Aileron control rods
40 Flap
41 First aid
42 Flares
43 Fuselage frame
44 Fuselage covering
45 Ammunition boxes, port
46 Ammunition boxes, st'b'd
47 Cartridge belts
48 Turret FN50 2, .303in
49 Smoke bombs
50 Fuselage structure
51 Elsan toilet
52 First aid
53 Emergency tools
54 Sliding door
55 Stabilizer
56 Fin
57 Directional static balance
58 Aerial

59 Rudder
60 Trim tab
61 Trim tab static balance
62 Elevator
63 Tab
64 Turret FN20, 4 .303in
65 Shell chute
66 Tailwheel
67 Fork
68 Wheel strut
69 Stabilizer structure
70 Rudder structure
71 Fin structure
72 Aerial
73 Turret FN, 2 .303in
74 Small calibre bombs
75 Bomb door jack
76 Rear bomb door
77 Split flap
78 Engine nacello rear,— hinged with flap
79 Rear spar
80 U/C door
81 U/C leg
82 Wheel
83 Aileron structure

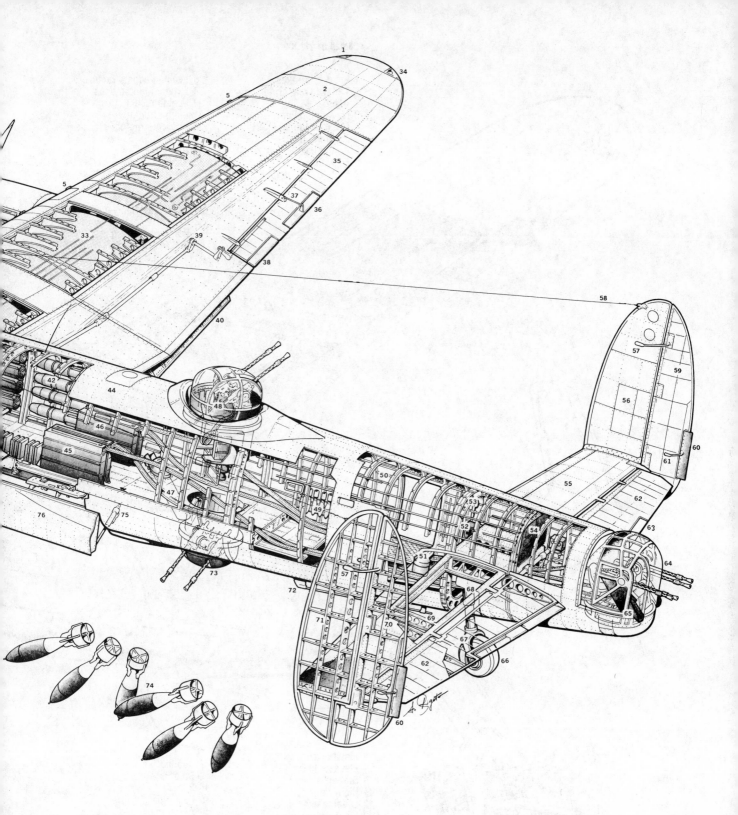

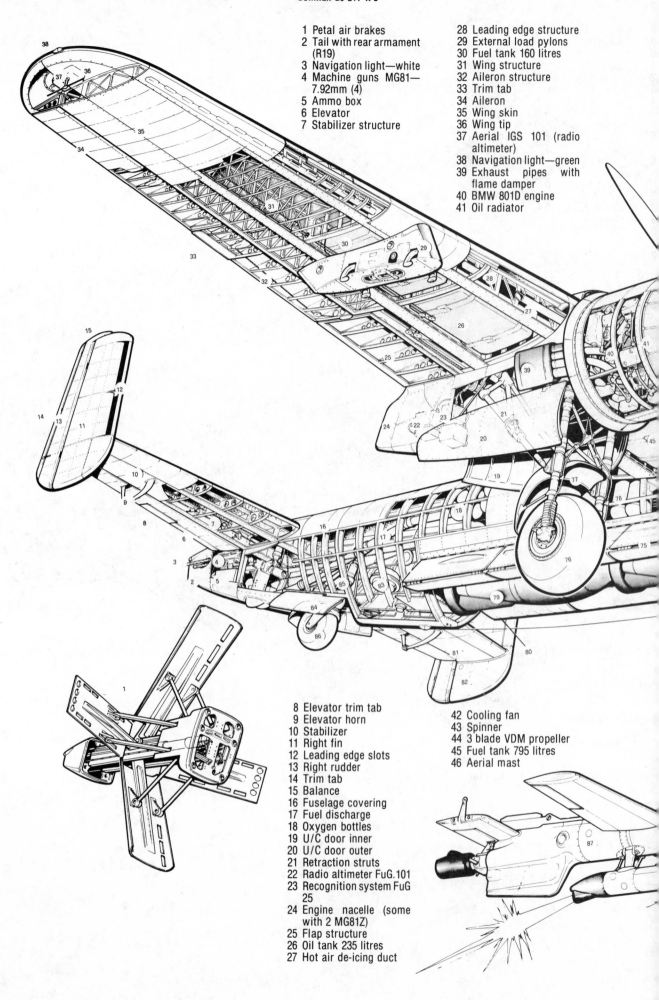

DORNIER Do 217 K-3

1 Petal air brakes
2 Tail with rear armament (R19)
3 Navigation light—white
4 Machine guns MG81— 7.92mm (4)
5 Ammo box
6 Elevator
7 Stabilizer structure

28 Leading edge structure
29 External load pylons
30 Fuel tank 160 litres
31 Wing structure
32 Aileron structure
33 Trim tab
34 Aileron
35 Wing skin
36 Wing tip
37 Aerial IGS 101 (radio altimeter)
38 Navigation light—green
39 Exhaust pipes with flame damper
40 BMW 801D engine
41 Oil radiator

8 Elevator trim tab
9 Elevator horn
10 Stabilizer
11 Right fin
12 Leading edge slots
13 Right rudder
14 Trim tab
15 Balance
16 Fuselage covering
17 Fuel discharge
18 Oxygen bottles
19 U/C door inner
20 U/C door outer
21 Retraction struts
22 Radio altimeter FuG.101
23 Recognition system FuG 25
24 Engine nacelle (some with 2 MG81Z)
25 Flap structure
26 Oil tank 235 litres
27 Hot air de-icing duct

42 Cooling fan
43 Spinner
44 3 blade VDM propeller
45 Fuel tank 795 litres
46 Aerial mast

46

47 Machine gun MH81 7.92mm
48 Dorsal gun stop
49 Turret with MG131 13mm
50 Ammunition box
51 Pilot's seat
52 Rearview periscope
53 Gunsight PV-1B
54 Machine gun MG131 13mm (or double MH81Z 7.92mm)
55 Control column and throttle quadrant
56 Shell clip and cartridge case recovery box and gunner's flat glass
57 Aiming system Lofte 7D
58 Port engine
59 Auxiliary tank
60 Retracting landing gear
61 Pitot tube
62 Navigation light—red

63 Tyre
64 Mudguard
65 Fork
66 U/C cross bracing structure
67 U/C door inner
68 U/C door outer
69 External load attachments
70 Door and access ladder
71 Ammunition box
72 Machine gun MG131 13mm
73 Aerial
74 Bomb SE 1000 1000kg
75 Bomb bay door

76 St'b'd U/C
77 Mudguard
78 Compressed air bottles
79 Bomb SC 1000 1000kg
80 Aerial
81 Port stabilizer
82 Port fin
83 Main compass
84 Tailwheel door
85 Wheel fork
86 Tailwheel
87 Henschel HS 293 guided self propelled bomb
88 Missile FX1400 Fritz X

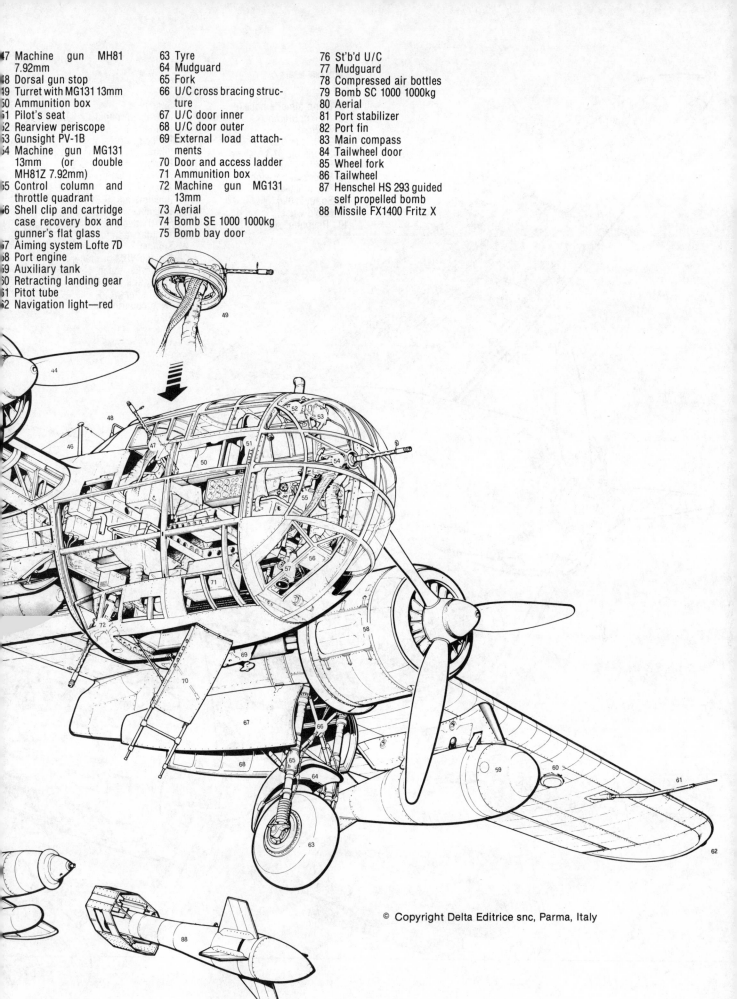

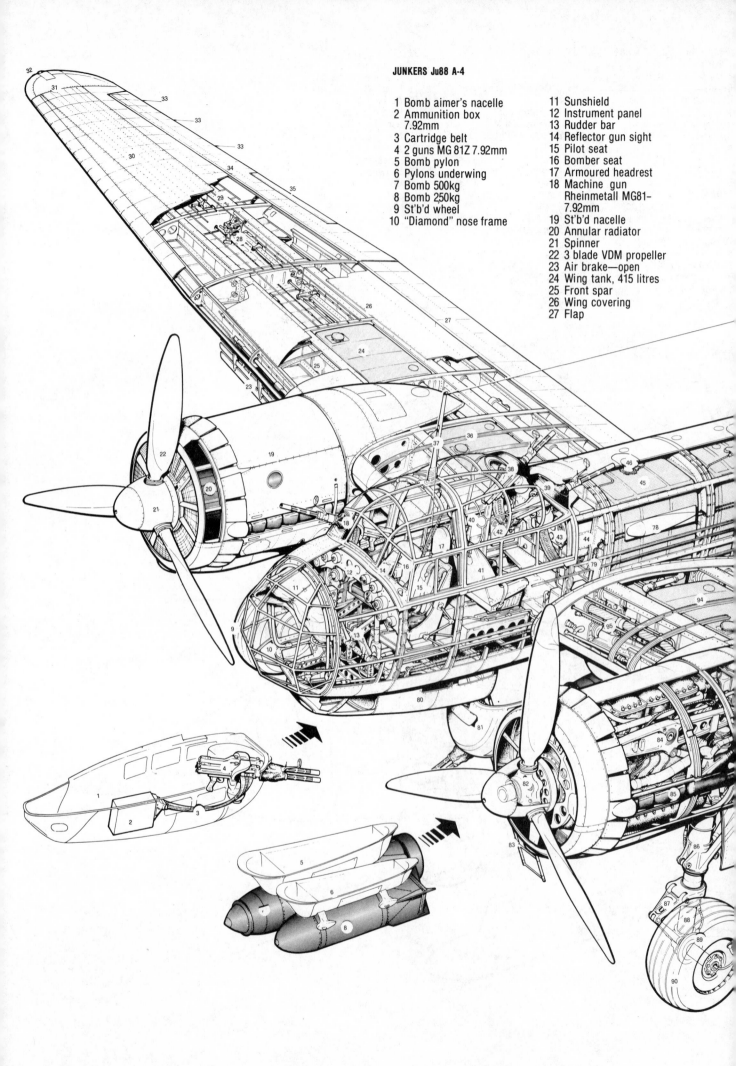

JUNKERS Ju88 A-4

1 Bomb aimer's nacelle
2 Ammunition box 7.92mm
3 Cartridge belt
4 2 guns MG 81Z 7.92mm
5 Bomb pylon
6 Pylons underwing
7 Bomb 500kg
8 Bomb 250kg
9 St'b'd wheel
10 "Diamond" nose frame
11 Sunshield
12 Instrument panel
13 Rudder bar
14 Reflector gun sight
15 Pilot seat
16 Bomber seat
17 Armoured headrest
18 Machine gun Rheinmetall MG81– 7.92mm
19 St'b'd nacelle
20 Annular radiator
21 Spinner
22 3 blade VDM propeller
23 Air brake—open
24 Wing tank, 415 litres
25 Front spar
26 Wing covering
27 Flap

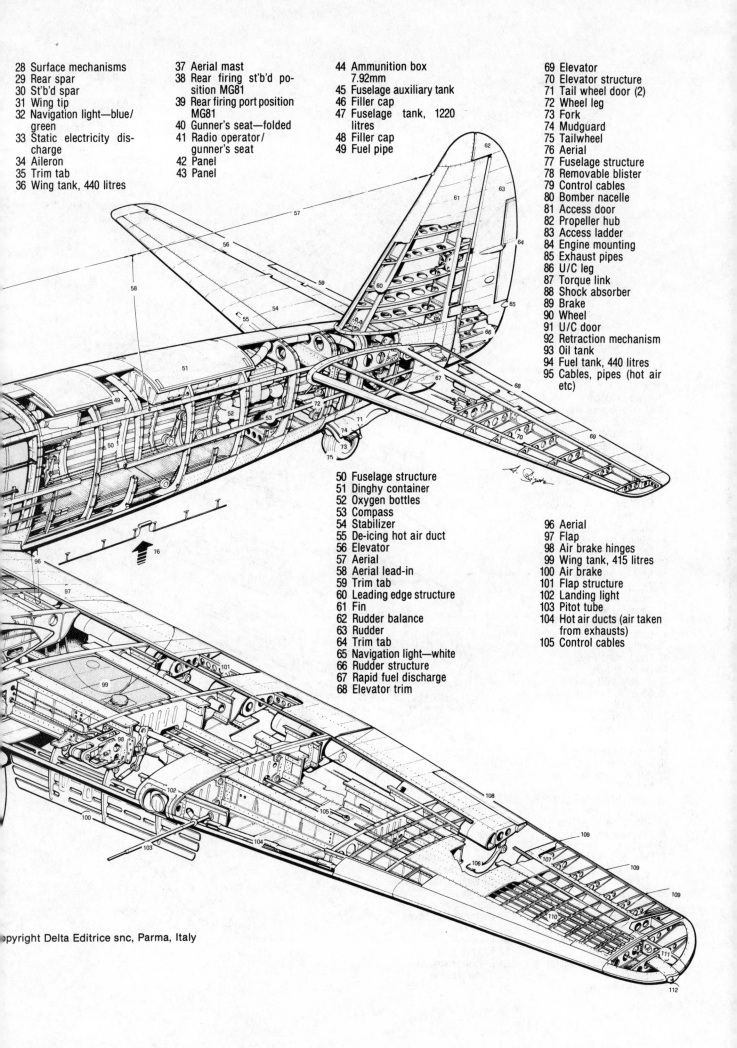

28 Surface mechanisms
29 Rear spar
30 St'b'd spar
31 Wing tip
32 Navigation light—blue/green
33 Static electricity discharge
34 Aileron
35 Trim tab
36 Wing tank, 440 litres

37 Aerial mast
38 Rear firing st'b'd position MG81
39 Rear firing port position MG81
40 Gunner's seat—folded
41 Radio operator/gunner's seat
42 Panel
43 Panel

44 Ammunition box 7.92mm
45 Fuselage auxiliary tank
46 Filler cap
47 Fuselage tank, 1220 litres
48 Filler cap
49 Fuel pipe

50 Fuselage structure
51 Dinghy container
52 Oxygen bottles
53 Compass
54 Stabilizer
55 De-icing hot air duct
56 Elevator
57 Aerial
58 Aerial lead-in
59 Trim tab
60 Leading edge structure
61 Fin
62 Rudder balance
63 Rudder
64 Trim tab
65 Navigation light—white
66 Rudder structure
67 Rapid fuel discharge
68 Elevator trim

69 Elevator
70 Elevator structure
71 Tail wheel door (2)
72 Wheel leg
73 Fork
74 Mudguard
75 Tailwheel
76 Aerial
77 Fuselage structure
78 Removable blister
79 Control cables
80 Bomber nacelle
81 Access door
82 Propeller hub
83 Access ladder
84 Engine mounting
85 Exhaust pipes
86 U/C leg
87 Torque link
88 Shock absorber
89 Brake
90 Wheel
91 U/C door
92 Retraction mechanism
93 Oil tank
94 Fuel tank, 440 litres
95 Cables, pipes (hot air etc)

96 Aerial
97 Flap
98 Air brake hinges
99 Wing tank, 415 litres
100 Air brake
101 Flap structure
102 Landing light
103 Pitot tube
104 Hot air ducts (air taken from exhausts)
105 Control cables

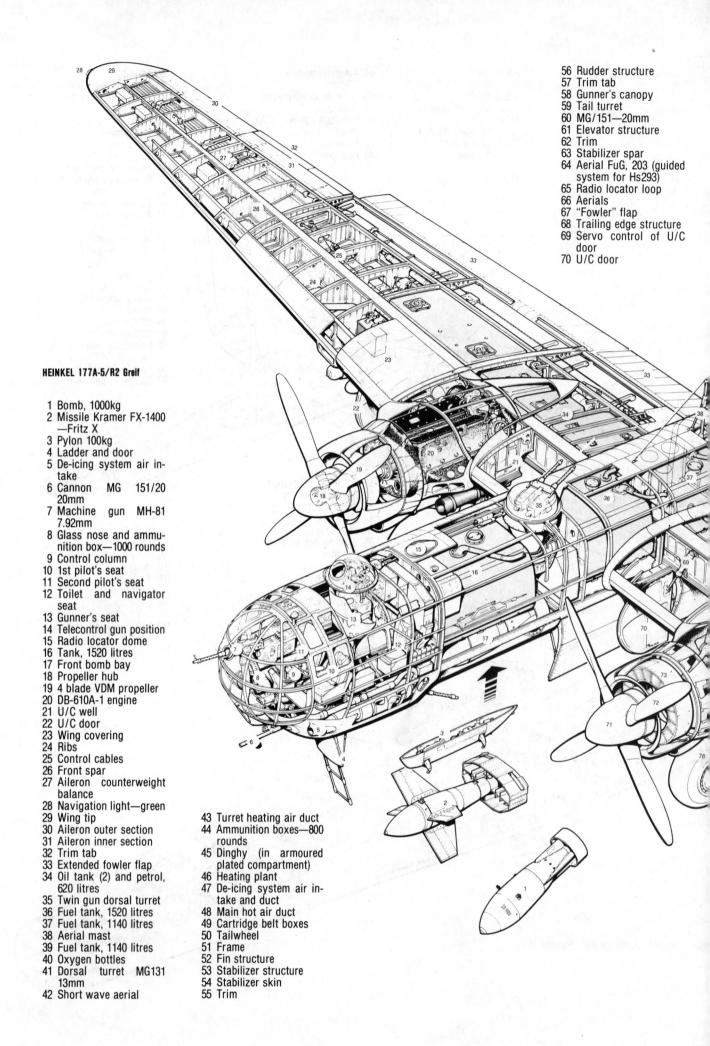

HEINKEL 177A-5/R2 Greif

1 Bomb, 1000kg
2 Missile Kramer FX-1400 —Fritz X
3 Pylon 100kg
4 Ladder and door
5 De-icing system air intake
6 Cannon MG 151/20 20mm
7 Machine gun MH-81 7.92mm
8 Glass nose and ammunition box—1000 rounds
9 Control column
10 1st pilot's seat
11 Second pilot's seat
12 Toilet and navigator seat
13 Gunner's seat
14 Telecontrol gun position
15 Radio locator dome
16 Tank, 1520 litres
17 Front bomb bay
18 Propeller hub
19 4 blade VDM propeller
20 DB-610A-1 engine
21 U/C well
22 U/C door
23 Wing covering
24 Ribs
25 Control cables
26 Front spar
27 Aileron counterweight balance
28 Navigation light—green
29 Wing tip
30 Aileron outer section
31 Aileron inner section
32 Trim tab
33 Extended fowler flap
34 Oil tank (2) and petrol, 620 litres
35 Twin gun dorsal turret
36 Fuel tank, 1520 litres
37 Fuel tank, 1140 litres
38 Aerial mast
39 Fuel tank, 1140 litres
40 Oxygen bottles
41 Dorsal turret MG131 13mm
42 Short wave aerial

43 Turret heating air duct
44 Ammunition boxes—800 rounds
45 Dinghy (in armoured plated compartment)
46 Heating plant
47 De-icing system air intake and duct
48 Main hot air duct
49 Cartridge belt boxes
50 Tailwheel
51 Frame
52 Fin structure
53 Stabilizer structure
54 Stabilizer skin
55 Trim

56 Rudder structure
57 Trim tab
58 Gunner's canopy
59 Tail turret
60 MG/151—20mm
61 Elevator structure
62 Trim
63 Stabilizer spar
64 Aerial FuG, 203 (guided system for Hs293)
65 Radio locator loop
66 Aerials
67 "Fowler" flap
68 Trailing edge structure
69 Servo control of U/C door
70 U/C door

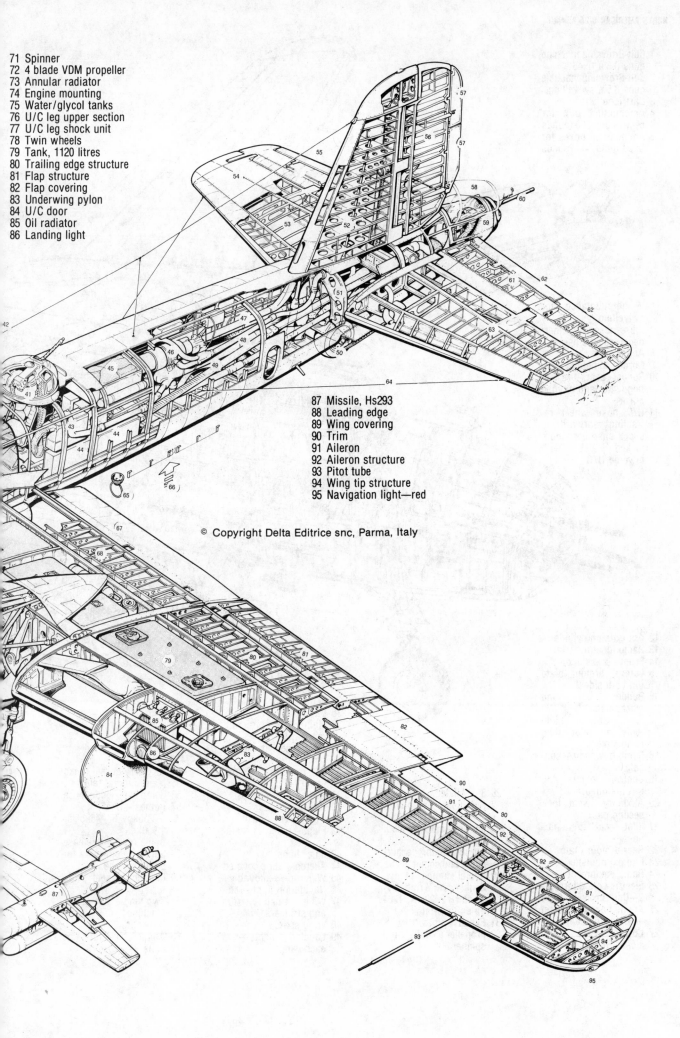

71 Spinner
72 4 blade VDM propeller
73 Annular radiator
74 Engine mounting
75 Water/glycol tanks
76 U/C leg upper section
77 U/C leg shock unit
78 Twin wheels
79 Tank, 1120 litres
80 Trailing edge structure
81 Flap structure
82 Flap covering
83 Underwing pylon
84 U/C door
85 Oil radiator
86 Landing light

87 Missile, Hs293
88 Leading edge
89 Wing covering
90 Trim
91 Aileron
92 Aileron structure
93 Pitot tube
94 Wing tip structure
95 Navigation light—red

© Copyright Delta Editrice snc, Parma, Italy

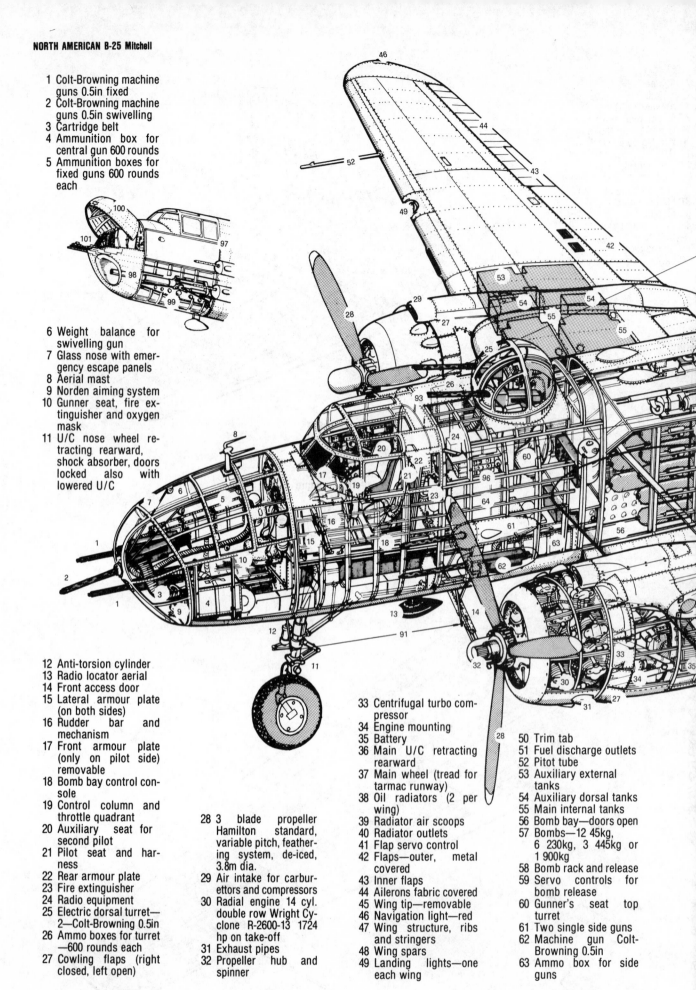

1 Colt-Browning machine guns 0.5in fixed
2 Colt-Browning machine guns 0.5in swivelling
3 Cartridge belt
4 Ammunition box for central gun 600 rounds
5 Ammunition boxes for fixed guns 600 rounds each

6 Weight balance for swivelling gun
7 Glass nose with emergency escape panels
8 Aerial mast
9 Norden aiming system
10 Gunner seat, fire extinguisher and oxygen mask
11 U/C nose wheel retracting rearward, shock absorber, doors locked also with lowered U/C

12 Anti-torsion cylinder
13 Radio locator aerial
14 Front access door
15 Lateral armour plate (on both sides)
16 Rudder bar and mechanism
17 Front armour plate (only on pilot side) removable
18 Bomb bay control console
19 Control column and throttle quadrant
20 Auxiliary seat for second pilot
21 Pilot seat and harness
22 Rear armour plate
23 Fire extinguisher
24 Radio equipment
25 Electric dorsal turret—2—Colt-Browning 0.5in
26 Ammo boxes for turret—600 rounds each
27 Cowling flaps (right closed, left open)

28 3 blade propeller Hamilton standard, variable pitch, feathering system, de-iced, 3.8m dia.
29 Air intake for carburettors and compressors
30 Radial engine 14 cyl. double row Wright Cyclone R-2600-13 1724 hp on take-off
31 Exhaust pipes
32 Propeller hub and spinner

33 Centrifugal turbo compressor
34 Engine mounting
35 Battery
36 Main U/C retracting rearward
37 Main wheel (tread for tarmac runway)
38 Oil radiators (2 per wing)
39 Radiator air scoops
40 Radiator outlets
41 Flap servo control
42 Flaps—outer, metal covered
43 Inner flaps
44 Ailerons fabric covered
45 Wing tip—removable
46 Navigation light—red
47 Wing structure, ribs and stringers
48 Wing spars
49 Landing lights—one each wing

50 Trim tab
51 Fuel discharge outlets
52 Pitot tube
53 Auxiliary external tanks
54 Auxiliary dorsal tanks
55 Main internal tanks
56 Bomb bay—doors open
57 Bombs—12 45kg, 6 230kg, 3 445kg or 1 900kg
58 Bomb rack and release
59 Servo controls for bomb release
60 Gunner's seat top turret
61 Two single side guns
62 Machine gun Colt-Browning 0.5in
63 Ammo box for side guns

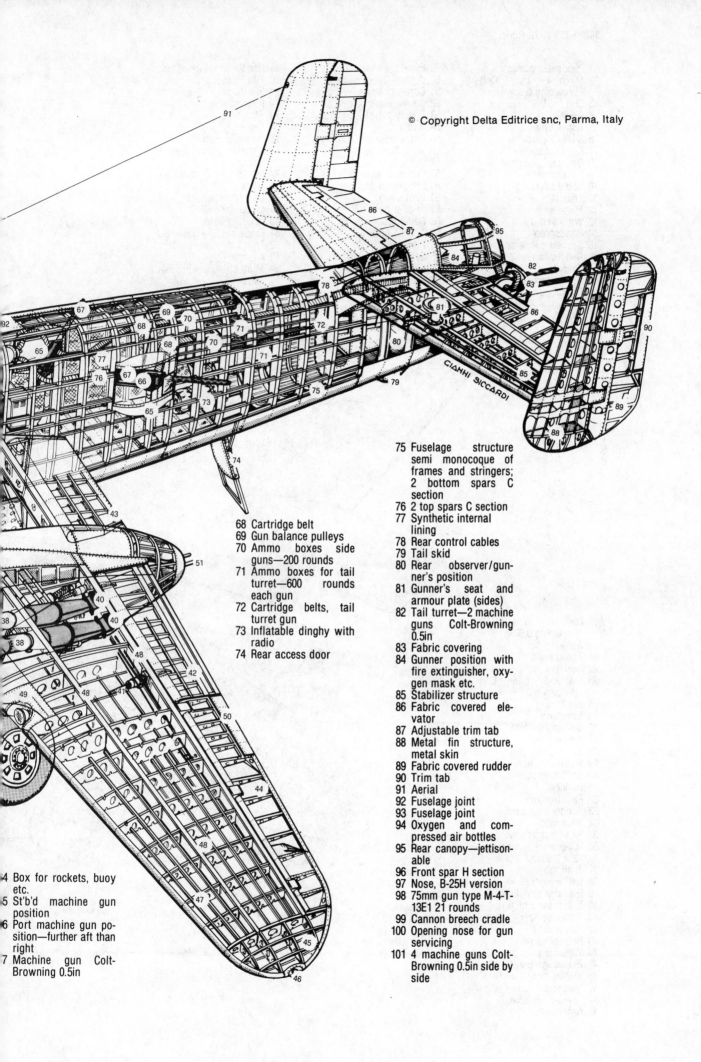

CIANHI SICCARDI

68 Cartridge belt
69 Gun balance pulleys
70 Ammo boxes side guns—200 rounds
71 Ammo boxes for tail turret—600 rounds each gun
72 Cartridge belts, tail turret gun
73 Inflatable dinghy with radio
74 Rear access door

4 Box for rockets, buoy etc.
5 St'b'd machine gun position
6 Port machine gun position—further aft than right
7 Machine gun Colt-Browning 0.5in

75 Fuselage structure semi monocoque of frames and stringers; 2 bottom spars C section
76 2 top spars C section
77 Synthetic internal lining
78 Rear control cables
79 Tail skid
80 Rear observer/gunner's position
81 Gunner's seat and armour plate (sides)
82 Tail turret—2 machine guns Colt-Browning 0.5in
83 Fabric covering
84 Gunner position with fire extinguisher, oxygen mask etc.
85 Stabilizer structure
86 Fabric covered elevator
87 Adjustable trim tab
88 Metal fin structure, metal skin
89 Fabric covered rudder
90 Trim tab
91 Aerial
92 Fuselage joint
93 Fuselage joint
94 Oxygen and compressed air bottles
95 Rear canopy—jettisonable
96 Front spar H section
97 Nose, B-25H version
98 75mm gun type M-4-T-13E1 21 rounds
99 Cannon breech cradle
100 Opening nose for gun servicing
101 4 machine guns Colt-Browning 0.5in side by side

1 Plexiglass nose
2 Machine gun Colt-Browning 0.5in
3 Gun feed
4 Aerial
5 Astrodome
6 3 blade propeller
7 Engine nacelle
8 De-icing system
9 Internal tank
10 St'b'd aileron
11 Trim tab
12 Metal skin
13 Whip aerial
14 Windscreen
15 Second pilot's seat
16 Bendix turret (2 × 0.5in guns)
17 Ammo boxes
18 Dorsal gun panel

49 Fuselage structure
50 Control cable guides
51 Control cables
52 Ammunition boxes
53 Sperry turret—2 × 0.5in
54 Radio
55 Radio operator's seat
56 Wing fairings
57 Bomb bay
58 Gunner's seat
59 Oxygen tanks
60 Pilot's seat
61 Rudder bar
62 Radio locator aerial
63 Access door
64 Pitot tube
65 Seat
66 Side gun 0.5mm
67 Bomber's seat
68 Norden aiming system

69 Bendix turret 2 × 0.5in
70 Filler cap
71 Front spar
72 Rear spar
73 Structure
74 Covering
75 Propeller hub
76 Variable pitch mechanism
77 GR-1820-97 Cyclone engine
78 Compressor duct
79 Compressor B22
80 Landing light
81 Flap structure (lowered)
82 Trim tab
83 Aileron
84 Multi stringer wing skin structure
85 Ribs
86 Navigation light
87 Wheel
88 Retracting arm
89 U/C wheel leg

19 Machine gun Colt-Browning 0.5in
20 Aerial
21 Aerial mast
22 Aerial
23 Machine gun Colt-Browning 0.5in
24 Fin fairing
25 Structure
26 De-icing system
27 Aerial
28 St'b'd stabilizer
29 St'b'd elevator
30 Stabilizer tip
31 De-icer
32 Fin structure
33 Rudder structure
34 Trim tab
35 Rear gunner's window
36 "Cheyenne" turret—2 × 2 0.5in
37 Trim tab
38 Left elevator
39 Elevator structure
40 Stabilizer structure
41 Port stabilizer
42 Tailwheel
43 Retraction jack
44 Wheel leg
45 Retraction pivot
46 Sliding door
47 Machine gun Colt-Browning 0.5in
48 Ammunition box

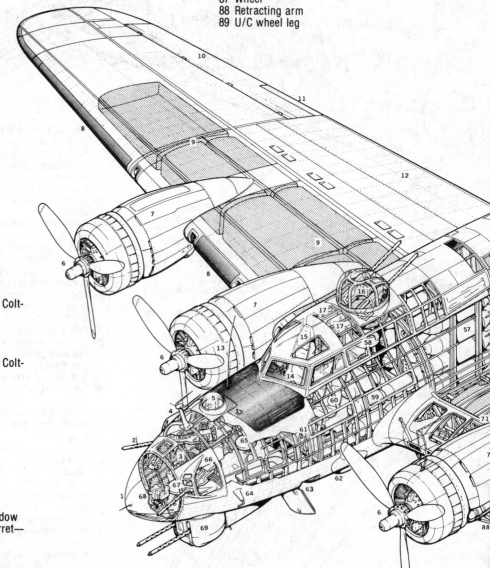

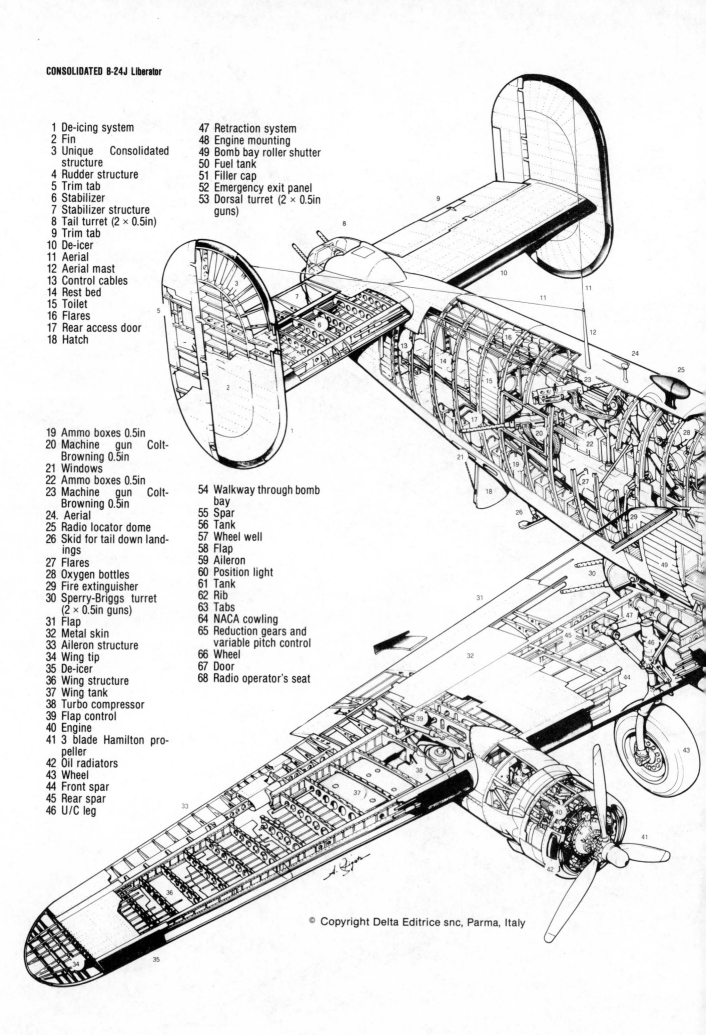

1 De-icing system
2 Fin
3 Unique   Consolidated
   structure
4 Rudder structure
5 Trim tab
6 Stabilizer
7 Stabilizer structure
8 Tail turret (2 × 0.5in)
9 Trim tab
10 De-icer
11 Aerial
12 Aerial mast
13 Control cables
14 Rest bed
15 Toilet
16 Flares
17 Rear access door
18 Hatch

47 Retraction system
48 Engine mounting
49 Bomb bay roller shutter
50 Fuel tank
51 Filler cap
52 Emergency exit panel
53 Dorsal turret (2 × 0.5in
   guns)

19 Ammo boxes 0.5in
20 Machine   gun   Colt-
   Browning 0.5in
21 Windows
22 Ammo boxes 0.5in
23 Machine   gun   Colt-
   Browning 0.5in
24. Aerial
25 Radio locator dome
26 Skid for tail down land-
   ings
27 Flares
28 Oxygen bottles
29 Fire extinguisher
30 Sperry-Briggs turret
   (2 × 0.5in guns)
31 Flap
32 Metal skin
33 Aileron structure
34 Wing tip
35 De-icer
36 Wing structure
37 Wing tank
38 Turbo compressor
39 Flap control
40 Engine
41 3 blade Hamilton pro-
   peller
42 Oil radiators
43 Wheel
44 Front spar
45 Rear spar
46 U/C leg

54 Walkway through bomb
   bay
55 Spar
56 Tank
57 Wheel well
58 Flap
59 Aileron
60 Position light
61 Tank
62 Rib
63 Tabs
64 NACA cowling
65 Reduction gears and
   variable pitch control
66 Wheel
67 Door
68 Radio operator's seat

© Copyright Delta Editrice snc, Parma, Italy

69 Communication
   passage
70 Auxiliary container
71 Bomb bay
72 Bomb bay access
   ladder
73 Frame
74 Battery
75 Cockpit floor
76 Co-pilot's seat
77 1st pilot's seat
78 Transparent canopy
79 Control column
80 Instrument panel
81 Rudder bar
82 Pitot tube
83 Astrodome

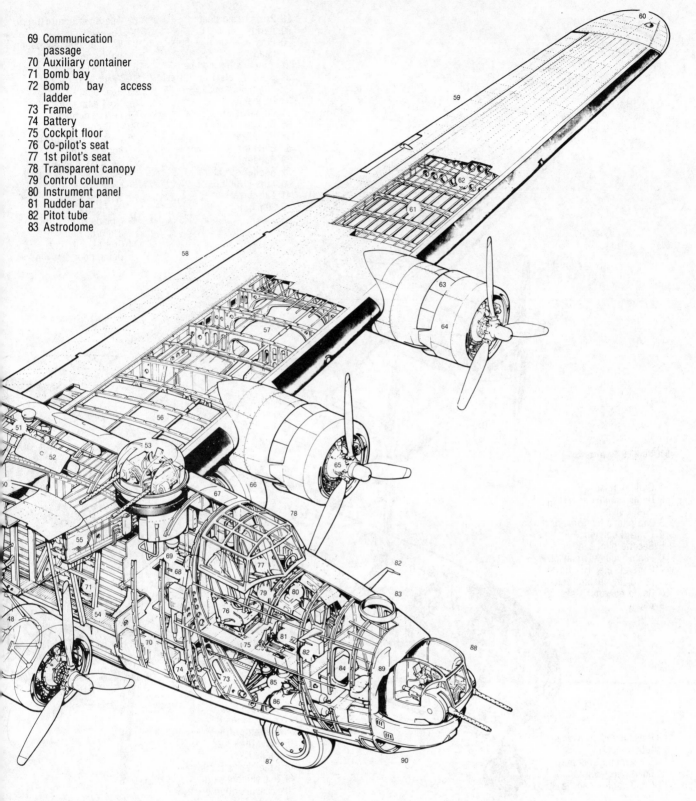

84 Window
85 Nose wheel leg
86 Mudguard
87 Nose wheel
88 Emmerson turret
   (2 × 0.5in guns)
89 Rest seat observer
90 Observer windows

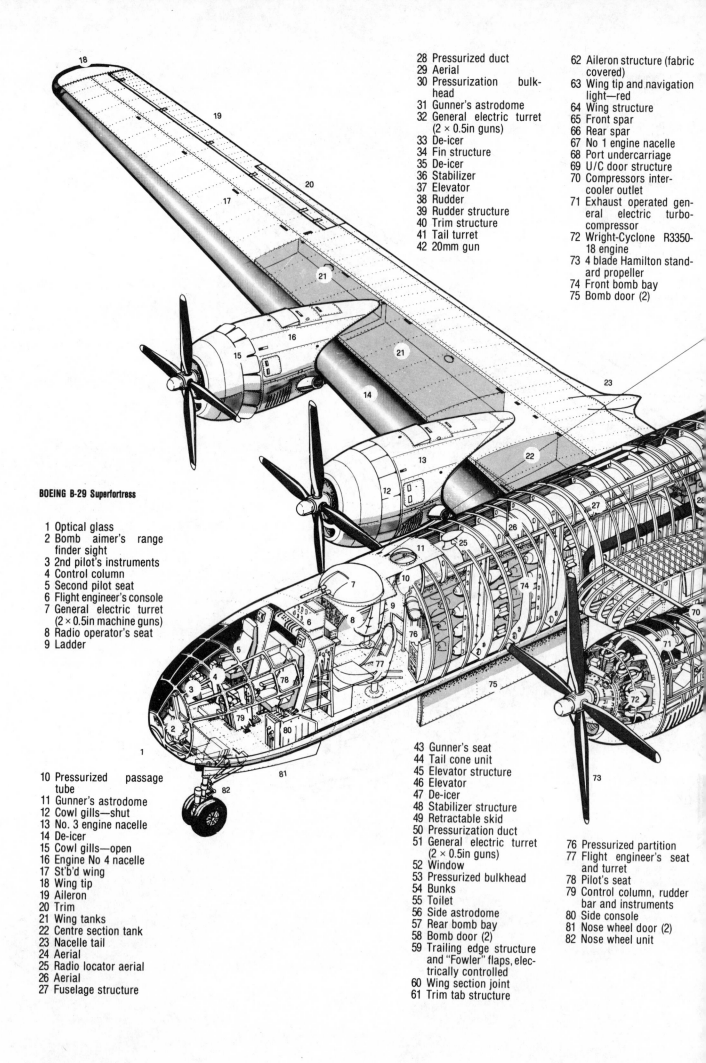

BOEING B-29 Superfortress

1 Optical glass
2 Bomb aimer's range finder sight
3 2nd pilot's instruments
4 Control column
5 Second pilot seat
6 Flight engineer's console
7 General electric turret (2 × 0.5in machine guns)
8 Radio operator's seat
9 Ladder

10 Pressurized passage tube
11 Gunner's astrodome
12 Cowl gills—shut
13 No. 3 engine nacelle
14 De-icer
15 Cowl gills—open
16 Engine No 4 nacelle
17 St'b'd wing
18 Wing tip
19 Aileron
20 Trim
21 Wing tanks
22 Centre section tank
23 Nacelle tail
24 Aerial
25 Radio locator aerial
26 Aerial
27 Fuselage structure

28 Pressurized duct
29 Aerial
30 Pressurization bulkhead
31 Gunner's astrodome
32 General electric turret (2 × 0.5in guns)
33 De-icer
34 Fin structure
35 De-icer
36 Stabilizer
37 Elevator
38 Rudder
39 Rudder structure
40 Trim structure
41 Tail turret
42 20mm gun

43 Gunner's seat
44 Tail cone unit
45 Elevator structure
46 Elevator
47 De-icer
48 Stabilizer structure
49 Retractable skid
50 Pressurization duct
51 General electric turret (2 × 0.5in guns)
52 Window
53 Pressurized bulkhead
54 Bunks
55 Toilet
56 Side astrodome
57 Rear bomb bay
58 Bomb door (2)
59 Trailing edge structure and "Fowler" flaps, electrically controlled
60 Wing section joint
61 Trim tab structure

62 Aileron structure (fabric covered)
63 Wing tip and navigation light—red
64 Wing structure
65 Front spar
66 Rear spar
67 No 1 engine nacelle
68 Port undercarriage
69 U/C door structure
70 Compressors inter-cooler outlet
71 Exhaust operated general electric turbo-compressor
72 Wright-Cyclone R3350-18 engine
73 4 blade Hamilton standard propeller
74 Front bomb bay
75 Bomb door (2)

76 Pressurized partition
77 Flight engineer's seat and turret
78 Pilot's seat
79 Control column, rudder bar and instruments
80 Side console
81 Nose wheel door (2)
82 Nose wheel unit

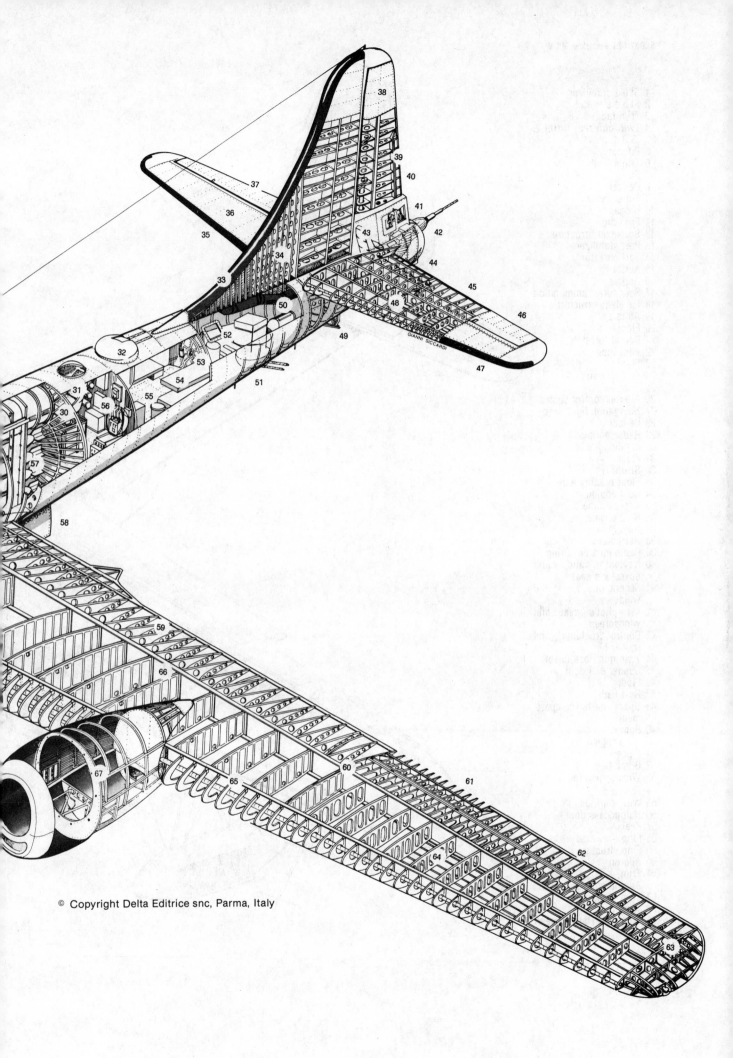

GIANNI SICCARDI

59

1 St'b'd stabilizer
2 St'b'd elevator
3 Trim tab
4 Twin gun rear turret 2, .303in
5 Rudder
6 Trims
7 Fin
8 De-icer
9 Fin structure
10 Hinges
11 First aid
12 Stabilizer structure
13 Port stabilizer
14 Port elevator
15 Aerial
16 Aerials
17 Rear turret ammunition
18 Fuselage structure
19 Aerials
20 Floor
21 Dorsal turret
22 Pitot tube
23 Flap
24 Port aileron
25 Trim
26 Aileron control cables
27 Navigation light—red
28 De-icer
29 Radar aerials
30 Landing lights
31 Float
32 Strut
33 Float bracing wire
34 No 1 engine
35 Access panels
36 No 2 engine
37 Aerials
38 Astrodome
39 Radio locator fairing
40 Navigator and radio operator's seat
41 Second pilot's seat and windows
42 1st pilot's seat and windscreen
43 Control column and rudder bar
44 Twin gun nose turret
45 Gunner exit door
46 Floor
47 Rest beds
48 Spare parts compartment
49 Bombs
50 No 3 engine
51 Pipes
52 Bomb bay
53 Wing structure
54 First aid
55 Wing fairings
56 Hull access door
57 Keel
58 Flap—lowered
59 Flap structure
60 Aileron
61 Trim
62 Aileron control cables
63 Trim structure
64 Wing tip
65 Navigation light—green

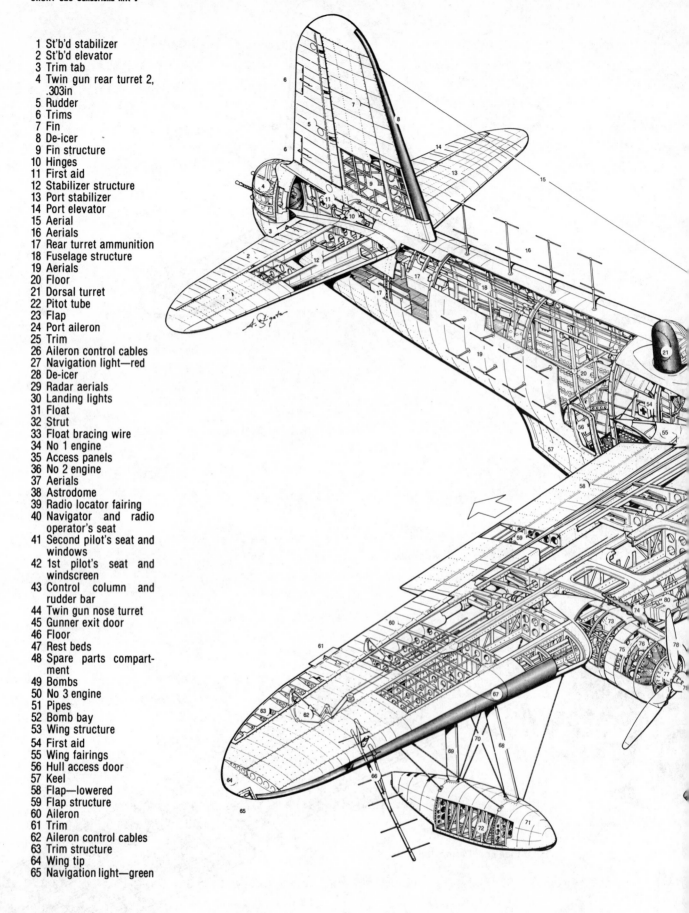

66 Aerials
67 De-icer
68 Front strut
69 Rear strut
70 Bracing wires
71 Float
72 Float structure
73 Oil tank
74 Exhaust pipes and dampers
75 Engine mounting
76 Exhaust pipes
77 Reduction gears
79 Hub and spinner
80 Oil radiators
81 Bombs

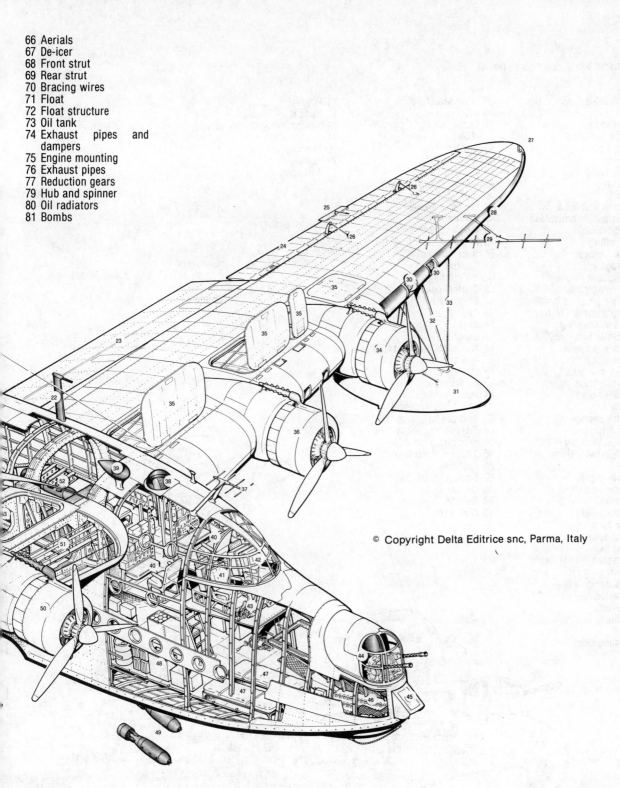

1 Retractable wing tip float
2 Float struts
3 Retraction strut
4 Wing tip
5 De-icer
6 St'b'd wing
7 Aileron
8 Trim
9 Perspex window with Venetian antisplash blind
10 Swivelling gun
11 Nose access for anchorage etc.
12 Antisplash stroke
13 Fastening rings
14 Anchor position inside
15 Compartment for front gunner, observer
16 Propeller hub
17 3 blade propeller
18 Reduction gears
19 NACA cowlings
20 Cowling flaps
21 Exhaust pipe
22 Aerial loop
23 Centre section
24 Reduction gear
25 Pratt & Whitney R-1830-SIC3-G twin Wasp engine
26 Cowling gills
27 Engine nacelle
28 De-icer
29 Landing light
30 Pitot tube
31 Front spar
32 Wing skin
33 Retracted float strut panel
34 Stabilizing float—retracted
35 Aileron
36 Aerial
37 Trim
38 Trailing edge

39 Wing structure
40 Rear spar
41 Depth charge bombs 205kg
42 Struts
43 Aerials
44 Trailing edge
45 Centre section wing tank
46 Engineer's seat
47 Float controls
48 Pylon structure
49 Engineer's controls
50 Superstructure
51 Cockpit fairing
52 1st pilot's seat
53 Control columns
54 Dashboard
55 Rudder bar
56 Keel
57 Bulkhead
58 Navigator and radio operator site
59 Luminous bouy
60 Bunks
61 Hull structure
62 St'b'd blister turret
63 Port blister turret
64 Swivelling Browning machine guns 0.5in
65 Toilet and partition
66 Hull step
67 Inspection passage
68 De-icer boor
69 De-icer
70 Stabilizer

71 Fin
72 Rudder
73 Navigation light—white
74 Stabilizer
75 Elevator
76 Rudder trim
77 Tail cone

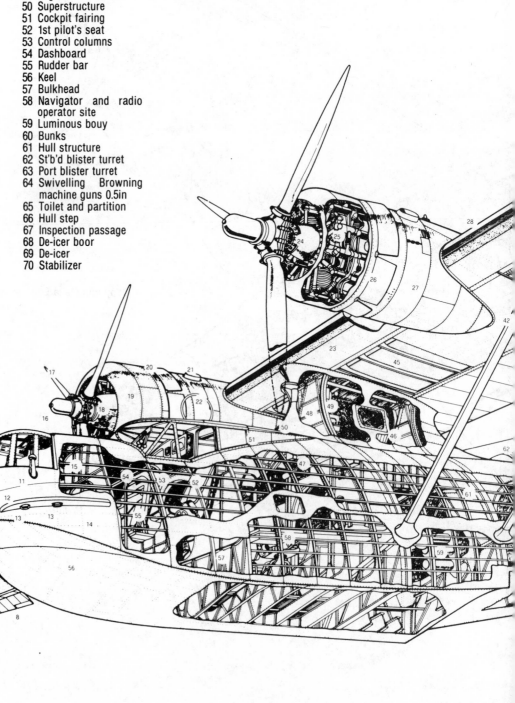

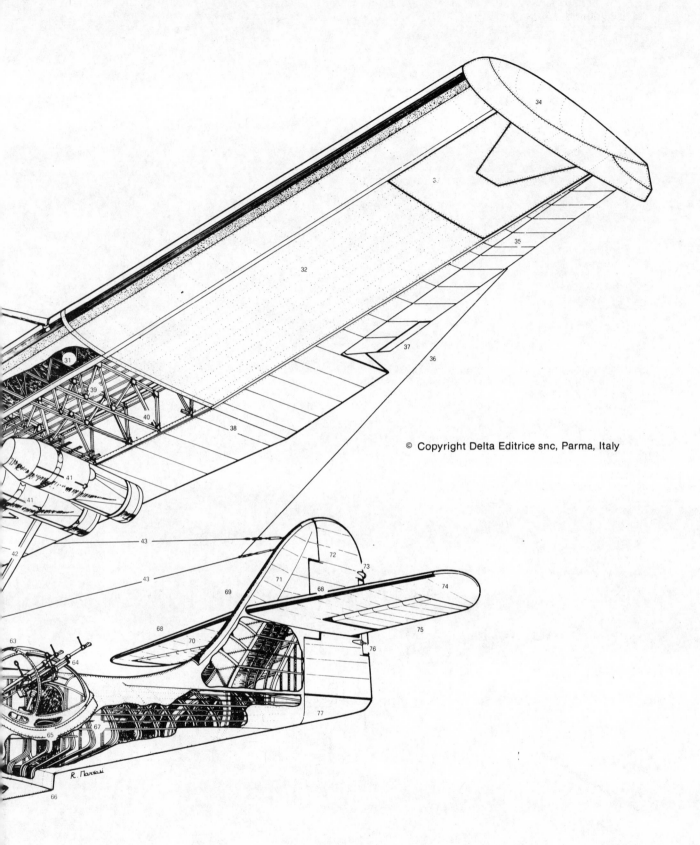

R. Narvai